Analysis of Resource Management in Complex Work Systems

Qinglian Lin

Analysis of Resource Management in Complex Work Systems

Using the Example of Sterile Goods Management in Hospitals

Springer

Qinglian Lin
School of Management
Xiamen University
Xiamen, Fujian
China

ISBN 978-981-10-2169-5 ISBN 978-981-10-2170-1 (eBook)
DOI 10.1007/978-981-10-2170-1

Library of Congress Control Number: 2016948234

Printed on acid-free paper

This Springer imprint is published by Springer Nature
The registered company is Springer Nature Singapore Pte Ltd.
The registered company address is: 152 Beach Road, #22-06/08 Gateway East, Singapore 189721, Singapore

Contents

Chapter 1
Introduction

In this chapter, it begins with the definition of "complexity" and introduces the complexity in the health care systems. After that, the changes in health care systems and challenges for hospital management are described. Health care is a complex system with emergent behavior, many interacting components, and inherent unpredictability. Decisions in health care should be made and implemented by multidisciplinary management teams. Health care systems face pressures to improve the efficiency in the provision of health services and to contain public spending, whilst maintaining the quality of the service. Hospitals, as one component of the health service organization, are seeking new paradigms to improve efficiency and effectiveness, especially for the use of resources.

1.1 Complexity of Health Care Systems

1.1.1 Definition of "Complexity"

Complexity tends to be used to characterize something with many parts in an intricate arrangement. However, complexity has turned out to be difficult to define. Many researchers use different definitions for the term "complexity". Some of these definitions are inappropriate, but a truly correct definition is difficult to obtain (Wikipedia 2013a; Heylighen 1996). Scherf (2003) who identified the following general characteristics of "complexity" (Podtschaske 2012):

- Abstract, i.e. complexity cannot be determined by empirically observable phenomena, but only by the mental evaluation of information perceived about the system;
- Gradual, i.e. one situation may be more complex than another;
- Collective or systemic, i.e. complexity does not refer to a single element, but rather a "structured unity".

Q. Lin, *Analysis of Resource Management in Complex Work Systems*,
DOI 10.1007/978-981-10-2170-1_1

Complexity theory has been applied in many fields, e.g. strategic management and organizational studies. Application areas include understanding how organizations cope with conditions of uncertainty, and how they adapt to the environments (Anderson 1999; Wikipedia 2013b). Complexity research combines approaches from different disciplines and seeks interdisciplinary insights (Mainzer 2008).

Asan (2009) summarized the characteristics of complex systems. Their main characteristics contain the structural and behavioral aspects (see Table 1.1).

Zimmerman et al. (1998) described complexity as "*a description of complex phenomena demonstrated in systems characterized by nonlinear interactive components, emergent phenomena, continuous and discontinuous change, and unpredictable outcomes. Complexity is usually understood in contrast to simple, linear and equilibrium-based system*".

According to Klir (1985), complexity is marked by an involvement of many interrelated parts, aspects, details, and notions, which are hard to fully understand. Ulrich and Probst (1991) presented complexity as "*the ability of a system to be able to assume a large number of different states within short time periods*" Flood (1987) illustrated that complexity is related to systems by the number and variety of elements and relationships, and by non-linearity, asymmetry and non-holonomic constraints. Complexity is also related to people by their notions and perceptions, and by their interests and capabilities.

Complex systems are systems with numerous components and interconnections, interactions or interdependence that are difficult to describe, understand, predict, manage, design, and change (Magee and de Weck 2004). Espinonsa and Walker (2011) described a complex system as: "*an open system, whose elements interact dynamically and nonlinearly, which exhibits unpredictable behaviours, is affected by positive and negative feedback loops and co-evolves with its environment*".

Systems are composed of a variety of elements that are connected by many various connections. All elements are combined in a system that creates a holistic unit, which is distinguishable and separable from other outward things (see Fig. 1.1) (Puhl 1999).

The simplest concept of relationships in systems forms linear causal chains. They present connections between system elements as simple lines that link together the causes and effects monocausally. It is assumed that an effect is due to a single cause. However, a cause can have different effects, and each of these effects can again have other effects. Causes and effects must not be linear, but rather can form feedback or feedback loops. This is how the networked causes and effects appear (Puhl 1999).

Systems can be divided into system hierarchies. Each system element can again be understood as being one of the elements of an existing system. If an element of a system itself is conceived as a system, while people form elements on a deeper level, it is called a subsystem. If multiple systems are combined into a more comprehensive system, then the term "super system" is used for this structure (Haberfellner et al. 1997).

Table 1.1 Defining the characteristics of complex systems

Numerousness	Numerousness refers to the number of components which make up the system and to the number of relationships and interactions between these components
Structural	
Variety	Variety refers to the number of different types of components in a system
Strength of interactions	The strength (significance) of interactions between the components of a system
Connective structure	The pattern of connectivity (interdependence) of the components in a system
Hierarchical structure	A system that has a hierarchical structure is composed of interrelated subsystems, each of which is hierarchical as well (has their own subsystems). In other words, in a hierarchical structure the components at a lower level are subsystems. They are interconnected and emerge into a higher level forming another subsystem
Behavioral	
Dynamism	Dynamism of a system refers to change and growth of the system in time
Nonlinearity	Nonlinearity means a small change may cause a large effect, a proportional effect, or no effect at all. However, in linear systems, effect is always directly proportional to cause Nonlinearity involves indeterminism (the behavior of a system cannot be predicted), multi-stability (the state of the system alternates between two or more exclusive states), aperiodicity (the system does not repeat the same behavior after some period), and irrationality (the behavior of the system lacks a normal cause effect relationship)
Far from equilibrium	Far from equilibrium means that the system is constantly changing and not returning to some prefixed state. This is a behavior of open systems which are continuously driven from the external environment
History	This characteristic is related to the memory of the system. Thus, prior states may have an influence on present and future states
Adaptive	The ability of complex systems to adjust themselves to their environment, mainly as a result of their ability to learn (from history) and change
Emergent structures	In complex systems the properties of the "wholes" cannot be reduced to the properties of the "parts". Such irreducible properties are called emergent. Thus, complex systems may exhibit behaviors that are unexpected, and which arises out of a multiplicity of relatively simple interactions of their parts
Self-organization	The spontaneous emergence of organization (consistency) due to the (local) interactions in the system
Evolution	The process of continuous change from a lower to a higher, or from a simpler to a more complex, or from a worse to a better state. Evolution is an opportunistic process

Complex systems are characterized from the perspective of system structures by two essential features: firstly, as high variety, understood as quantity and variety of different elements in the system, and secondly, as high networking, understood as the amount and variety of different relationships between elements in the system (Puhl 1999).

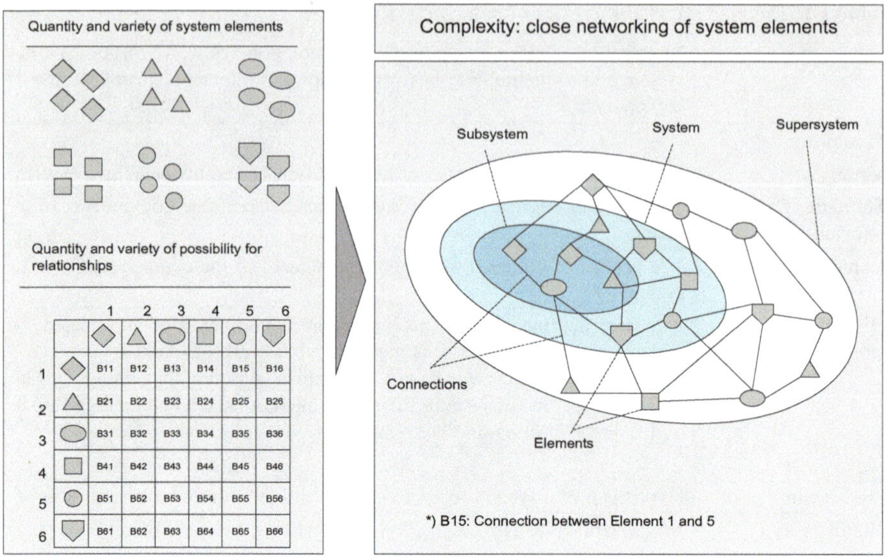

Fig. 1.1 Networking—system structure. *Source* Puhl (1999)

1.1.2 Complexity in the Health Care System

A complex system is characterized by a large number of individual factors, and the relationships of their dynamic effect. The individuality of patients, ethical issues, and the dynamics of diseases make the health care system complex (Krallmann 1994; Probst and Gomez 1991; Ulrich and Probst 1991; Marsolek 2003). Runciman et al. (2007) discussed health care as a complex system with emergent behavior, with many interacting components, and an inherent unpredictability. Effken (2002) viewed health care systems as dynamic complex socio-technical systems. Katerndahl et al. (2010) stated that health care complexity comprises "*multiple, dynamic components interacting in non-linear, unpredictable way.*" Health care complexity has increased because of the interaction of multiple factors. Hollnagel and Woods (2005) summarized the great number of factors which are the source of complexity in health care systems as personal factors, technology and tool factors, team factors, environmental factors, and organizational factors, etc.

There are three main inter-related aspects of health care complexity: medical complexity, situation complexity, and system complexity (Kuipers et al. 2011). After analyzing the complexity of health care, the factors associated with health care complexity and the responses to factors associated with health care complexity have been identified (see Fig. 1.2).

The complexity in health care systems is reflected in increasing health care costs. It affects the quality and outcomes of care (Kuipers et al. 2011; De Jonge et al. 2006). As a result of the complexity in health care systems, the decisions in health care should be made and implemented by multidisciplinary management teams

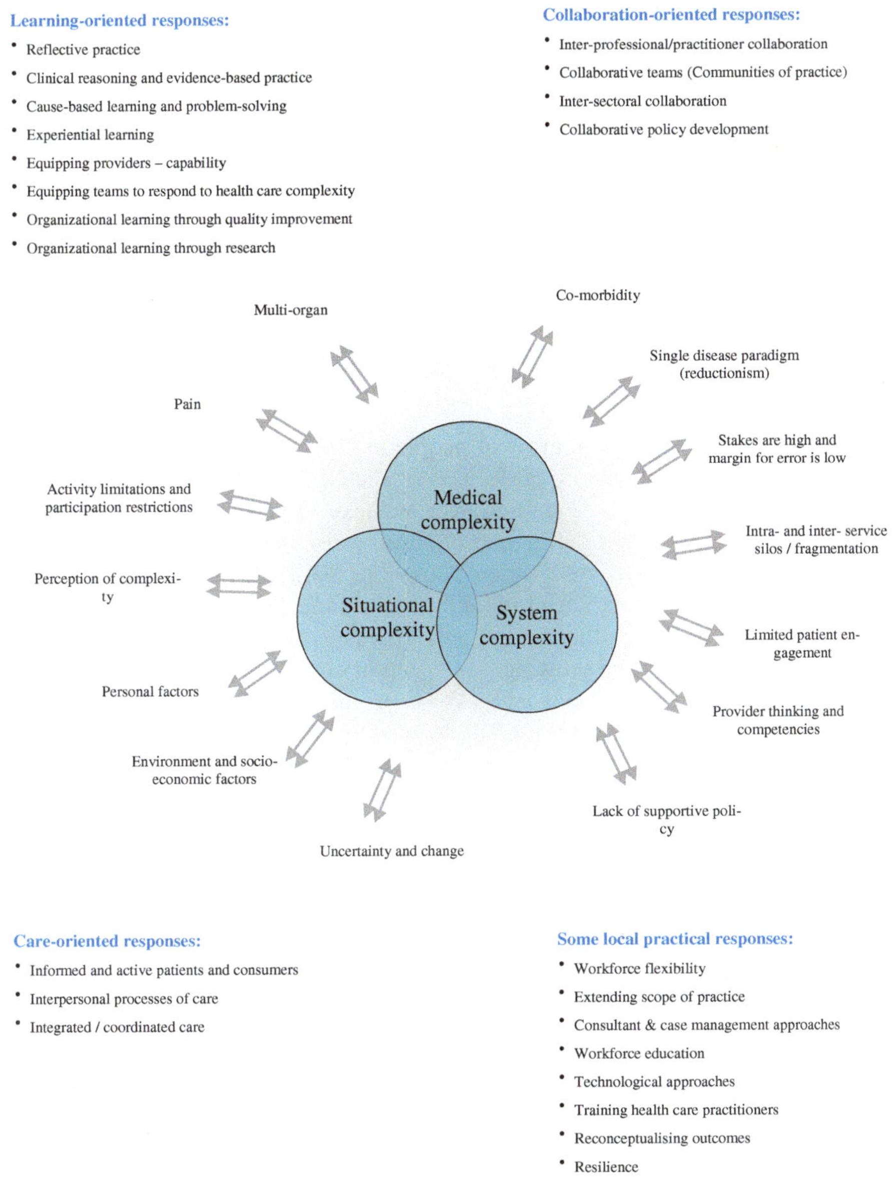

Fig. 1.2 Responses to factors associated with health care complexity. *Source* Kuipers et al. (2011)

(Baxter 2010). Also a multidisciplinary team is important for the patient treatmen (Podtschaske 2012). Medical decision making (see Appendix 1) or decision making in health care systems are both complicated due to the complexity.

1.2 Changes in Health Care Systems

The health care industry is facing a period of significant change. Ageing populations, new therapeutic possibilities and rising expectations have made the organization and provision of health care much more complex. Having an ageing population is an issue which numerous countries have faced in recent years. According to a statistical report, reduced birthrates and increased life expectancy will lead to rising financial expenditure which will in turn influence social development. An increase in life expectancy causes a worldwide demographic change. Demographic development is a major challenge, and is associated with fundamental changes in the existing structures in all areas of society. These changes affect primarily the current and future supply of health care (Rechel et al. 2006; Bloom et al. 2011; Podtschaske 2012; Pieper and Kolankowska 2011).

In the next 40 years, the number of people in Germany aged 65 and over will increase from approximately 15–30 %. It is predicted that the number of people in need of care will increase by 1 million over the next 20 years. This increase in the number of older people and the burden of chronic diseases will have a substantial impact on health care systems (Ulrich 2004; Liu 2012; Schultz et al. 2001). In China, the number of people aged 65 and over is more than 100 million in 2010, and will increase to 200 million in the next 40 years (NBSC 2013).

Health care is a large and growing proportion of our economy. More than $1 out of every $6 spent on final goods and services in the U.S. economy went into the health sector. In 2020, the share of GDP devoted to health care will be $1 in every $5. In recent decades, health care expenditure has grown very significantly in most developed countries (Folland et al. 2013; NHE Projections 2011–2021; Hernández de Cos and Moral-Benito 2011). Figure 1.3 shows the health care spending as a share of GDP from 1970 to 2010 in Germany, Japan, and United States.

The share of health expenditure is projected to rise sharply and will have disastrous implications for government budgets. It will increase the budget deficit. Slowing the growth of health care costs will have an economic impact on our society. Therefore, there are pressures to control the cost of health care, and to demonstrate the value of the services delivered. Health care systems aim to improve efficiency in the provision of health services and to contain public spending, whilst maintaining the quality of service. Managers are looking for ways to increase the efficiency of health care delivery, and to allocate resources to improve value in health care. Efficient resource utilization is now the fundamental challenge in health care management (Fraser et al. 2008; De Mast et al. 2011).

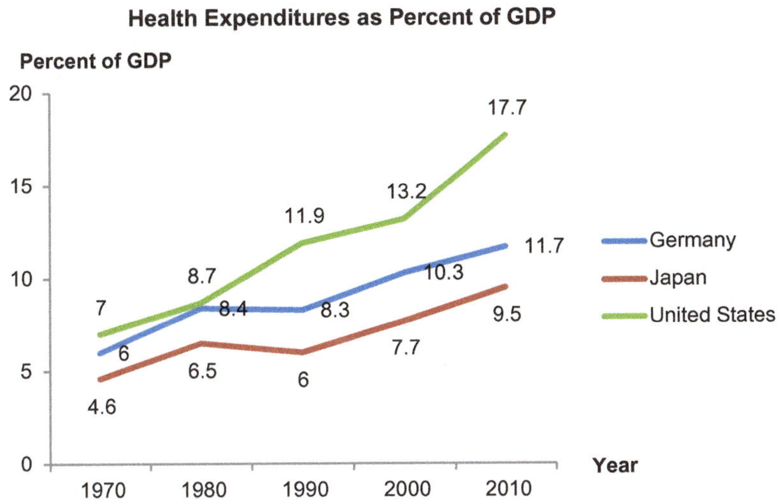

Fig. 1.3 Health expenditures as percent of GDP in Germany, Japan, and United States. *Source* Organization for economic cooperation and development (OECP) Health Care Data 2012

1.3 Challenges for Hospital Management

Providing greater value is a challenge for all health services organizations, and for the professionals associated with them. The Pew Commission Report on Education for the Health Professions noted that (Shortell and Kaluzny 2000):

> Health services management will become even more challenging, because it is the point where increasing service demands, cost containment strategies, inter-professional tensions, technological change pressures, guidelines implementation, and quality improvement mandates all converges. The managerial function in health services is unique because of the relative autonomy of providers and the complexity of assessing the quality of the services rendered.

Hospitals, as one component of the health service organization, are also facing the challenge to create value for an increasingly diverse and demanding population (Shortell and Kaluzny 2000). In recent years, a number of developments in the hospital environment have created many challenges for hospital management, requiring hospitals to change their strategies, structure, systems, as well as the way they provide health care. Hospitals, as complex organizations, are seeking new paradigms that will improve efficiency and effectiveness, especially the use of resources (Heine and Maddox 2010; Abernethy and Stoelwinder 1990).

Hospital costs account for over 30 % of national health care expenditure. In some countries this can be as high as 50 % (McKee and Healy 2000). As the health care expenditure increases, attempts to control hospital costs become more important. Lower prices, greater availability, and improved innovation and quality are welcome to consumers (patients). In an increasingly competitive, cost-conscious environment, hospitals are facing pressure: (1) to contain costs while simultaneously improving patient care and service; (2) to restructure through mergers, participation in hospital networks, and other partnerships; (3) to respond quickly to new incentives and opportunities (Folland et al. 2013; Lee and Ralph 2004; Frost and Sullivan 2011).

In this challenging environment, hospital administrators are responsible for making sure that hospitals operate efficiently whilst providing quality medical care for patients. As they are the most complex of organizations, hospital managers must continuously improve the level of teamwork, and ensure effective coordination and communication within and amongst teams within the organization (Freel 2012; Heine and Maddox 2010).

Appendix 1: Overview of Medical Decision Making

See Fig. 1.4.

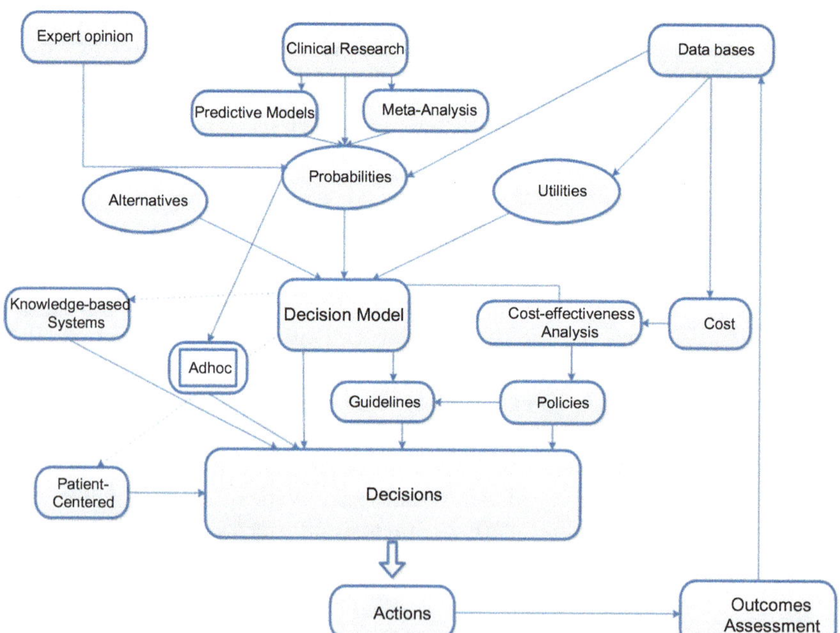

Fig. 1.4 Overview of medical decision making

References

Abernethy, M. A., & Stoelwinder, J. U. (1990). Physicians and resource management in hospitals: An empirical investigation. *Financial Accountability & Management, 6*(1), 17–31.

Anderson, P. (1999). Complexity theory and organization science. *Organization Science, 10*(3), 216–232.

Asan, S. S. (2009). A methodology based on theory of constraints' thinking processes for managing complexity in the supply chain. Dissertation, Technischen Universität Berlin, der Fakultät V – Verkehrs- und Maschinensysteme, Berlin.

Baxter, G. (2010). *White paper: Complexity in health care*. The UK National Research and Training Initiative. Retrieved April 6, 2013, from http://lscits.cs.bris.ac.uk/docs/Complexity%2Bin%2BHealth%2BCare.pdf

Bloom, D. E., Boersch-Supan, A., McGee, P., & Seike, A. (2011). *Population aging: Facts, challenges, and responses. Program on the global demography of aging*. Retrieved January 25, 2013, from http://www.hsph.harvard.edu/pgda/WorkingPapers/2011/PGDA_WP_71.pdf

De Jonge, P., Huyse, F. J., & Stiefel, F. C. (2006). Case and care complexity in the medically ill. *Medical Clinics of North America, 90*(4), 679–692.

De Mast, J., Kemper, B., Does, R. J. M. M., Mandjes, M., & van der Bijl, Y. (2011). Process improvement in healthcare: Overall resource efficiency. *Quality and Reliability Engineering International, 27*, 1095–1106.

Effken, J. (2002). Different lenses, improved outcomes: A new approach to the analysis and design of healthcare systems. *International Journal of Medical Informatics, 65*, 59–74.

Espinonsa, A., & Walker, J. (2011). *A complexity approach to sustainability: Theory and application*. London: Imperial College Press.

Flood, R. L. (1987). Complexity: A definition by construction of a conceptual framework. *Systems Research, 4*(3), 177–185.

Folland, S., Goodman, A. C., & Stano, M. (2013). *The economics of health and health care* (7th ed.). New Jersey: Pearson Education Inc.

Fraser, I., Encinosa, W., & Glied, S. (2008). Improving efficiency and value in health care: Introduction. *Health Services Research, 43*(5), 1781–1786.

Freel, M. (2012). *5 challenges hospital administrators must overcome to succeed in today's rapidly changing industry*. Retrieved February 9, 2013, from http://www.beckershospitalreview.com/hospital-management-administration/5-challenges-hospital-administrators-must-overcome-to-succeed-in-todays-rapidly-changing-industry.html

Frost, T. J., & Sullivan, D. M. (2011). *New opportunities for hospitals to improve efficiency and patient outcomes: The case of EXPAREL. A long-acting, non-opioid local analgesic. 50 years of growth, innovation and leadership*. Retrieved March 17, 2013, from https://www.google.de/url?sa=t&rct=j&q=&esrc=s&source=web&cd=4&cad=rja&ved=0CE0QFjAD&url=http%3A%2F%2Fwww.frost.com%2Fprod%2Fservlet%2Fcpo%2F252218999&ei=ODbRUbz1LMrNtQbZxICYDA&usg=AFQjCNEck1_P_u4nyOmwFkiUQboJUxlRdQ&sig2=OW9-_xNXREVIG955jMNdoQ&bvm=bv.48572450,d.Yms

Haberfellner, R., Nagel, P., Becker, M., Büchel, A., & von Massow, H. (1997). Systems engineering: Methodik und Praxis. 9. Verbesserte Auflage (W.F. Daenzer, & F. Huber, Hrsg.). Zuerich: Verl. Industrielle Organisation.

Heine, R. P., & Maddox, E. N. (2010). Hospital management reform: A step of healthcare reform. *Journal of Management and Marketing Research*. Retrieved February 9, 2013, from http://www.aabri.com/manuscripts/10443.pdf

Hernández de Cos, P., & Moral-Benito, E. (2011). *Health care expenditure in the OECD countries: Efficiency and regulation*. Retrieved April 4, 2013, from http://www.bde.es/f/webbde/SES/Secciones/Publicaciones/PublicacionesSeriadas/DocumentosOcasionales/11/Fich/do1107e.pdf

Heylighen, F. (1996). *What is complexity?* Retrieved April 5, 2013, from http://pespmc1.vub.ac.be/COMPLEXI.html

Hollnagel, E., & Woods, D. D. (2005). *Joint cognitive systems: Foundations of cognitive systems engineering*. Boca Raton: CRC Press.
Klir, G. J. (1985). Complexity: Some general observations. *Systems Research, 2*(2), 131–140.
Katerndahl, D., Parchman, M., & Wood, R. (2010). Trends in the perceived complexity of primary health care: A secondary analysis. *Journal of Evaluation in Clinical Practice, 16*(5), 1002–1008.
Krallmann, H. (1994). *Systemanalyse im Unternehmen – Geschaeftprozessoptimierung, partizipative Vorgehensmodelle, objektorientierte Analyse*. Muenchen: Oldenbourg Verlag.
Kuipers, P., Kendall, E., Ehrlich, C., et al. (2011). *Complexity and health care: health practitioner workforce services, roles, skills and training, to respond to patients with complex needs*. ClinEdQ, Queensland Health 2011. Retrieved March 15, 2013, from http://www.health.qld.gov.au/clinedq/Documents/CaHCHPWSRSTRPCN.pdf
Lee, R., & Ralph, R. (2004). Improving resource efficiency through management science. *Journal of Healthcare Management Publisher*. Retrieved January 22, 2013, from http://www.biomedsearch.com/article/Improving-resource-efficiency-through-management/122812090.html
Liu, H. L. (2012). Arbeitswissenschaftliches Modell zur nutzerorientierten Gestaltung technischer Produkte fuer Menschen mit krankheitsbedingten Einschraenkungen am Beispiel von Sanitaerprodukten. Dissertation, Technischen Universitaet Berlin, der Fakultaet V- Verkehrs- und Maschinensysteme, Berlin.
Magee, C., & de Weck, O. (2004). Complex system classification. In: *Fourteenth Annual International Symposium of the International Council on Systems Engineering*. Retrieved April 10, 2013, from http://strategic.mit.edu/docs/3_36_INCOSE2004_complexsys.pdf
Mainzer, K. (2008). *Komplexität. UTB Profile*. Wilhelm Fink Verlag: Paderborn.
Marsolek, I. (2003). Entwicklung einer arbeitswissenschaftlichen Methodik zur Analyse und Optimierung von komplexen Prozessfluessen im Arbeitssystem Krankenhaus. Dissertation, Technischen Universität Berlin, der Fakultät V - Verkehrs- und Maschinensysteme, Berlin.
McKee, M., & Healy, J. (2000). The role of the hospital in a changing environment. *Bulletin of the World Health Organization, 78*(6), 803–810.
NBSC—National Bureau of Statistics of China. Retrieved March 20, 2013, from http://www.stats.gov.cn/tjgb/rkpcgb/qgrkpcgb/t20110428_402722232.htm
NHE Projections 2011–2021. Retrieved March 2, 2013, from http://www.cms.gov/Research-Statistics-Data-and-Systems/Statistics-Trends-and-Reports/NationalHealthExpendData/Downloads/Proj2011PDF.pdf
Pieper, C., & Kolankowska, I. (2011). Health care transition in Germany—Standardization of procedures and improvement actions. *Journal of Multidisciplinary Healthcare, 4*, 215–221.
Podtschaske, B. (2012). Analyse and Gestaltung komplexer Arbeitssysteme am Beispiel der Patientenversorgung. Dissertation, Technischen Universität Berlin, der Fakultät VII – Wirschaft und Management, Berlin.
Probst, G. J. B., & Gomez, P. (1991). Die Methodik des Vernetzten Denkens zur Loesung komplexer Probleme. In: G. J. B. Probst & P. Gomez (Hrsg.), Vernetztes Denken – Ganzheitliches Fuehren in der Praxis. 2. Erweiterte Auflage. Wiesbaden: Gabler Verlag.
Puhl, H. (1999). Komplexitätsmanagement - Ein Konzept zur ganzheitlichen Ergassung, Plannung und Regelung der Komplexität in Unternehmensprozessen. Dissertation, Kaiserslautern Universität, Fertigungstechnik und Betriebsorganisation, Hannover.
Rechel, B., Dubois, C. A., & Mckee, M. (2006). *The health care workforce in Europe: Learning from experience. European observatory on health systems and policies*. Retrieved January 10, 2013, from http://www.euro.who.int/__data/assets/pdf_file/0008/91475/E89156.pdf
Runciman, B., Merry, A., & Walton, M. (2007). *Safety and ethics in healthcare: A guide to getting it right*. Aldershot: Ashgate Publishing.
Scherf, O. (2003). Komplexität aus systemischer Sicht. Dissertation, Universität St. Gallen, Hochschule für Wirtschafts-, Rechts- und Sozialwissenschaften (HSG), St. Gallen.
Schultz, E., Leidl, R., & König, H. H. (2001). Starker Anstieg der Pflegebedürftigkeit zu erwarten: Vorausschätzungen bis 2020 mit Ausblick auf 2050. *Wochenbericht, 68*(5), 65–77.

Shortell, S. M., & Kaluzny, A. D. (2000). Organization theory and health services management. In S. M. Shortell & A. D. Kaluzny (Eds.), *Health care management: Organization design and behavior* (4th ed.). New York: Delmar.

Ulrich, H., & Probst, G. J. B. (1991). *Anleitung zum ganzheitlich Denken und Handeln: Ein Brevier für Führungskräfte* (3rd ed.). Bern: Haupt Verlag.

Ulrich, R. E. (2004). Demographic change in Germany and implications for the health system. *J Public Health, 13*(1), 10–15.

Wikipedia. (2013a). *Complexity*. Retrieved June 3, 2013, from http://en.inforapid.org/index.php?search=Complexity

Wikipedia. (2013b). *Complexity theory and organizations*. Retrieved September 15, 2013, from http://en.wikipedia.org/wiki/Complexity_theory_and_organizations

Zimmerman, B., Lindberg, C., & Plsek, P. (1998). *Edgeware: Insights from complexity science for health care leaders*. Texas: VHA Inc.

Chapter 2
Research Problem and Aims

2.1 Research Problem

The health care system is subject to a significant change because of demographic developments. It is under pressure to improve efficiency in the provision of health services, especially the efficient allocation of resources. The provision of health care services is one of the largest and most complex of issues. It involves making decisions about the planning and management of health care resources (Harper 2002). Traditional decision making methods cannot guarantee the required comprehensiveness and adaptability of the complex work systems. In a complex system there are numerous components and interconnections, and interdependence which are difficult to describe, understand, and manage. They comprise a variety of elements and a large number of uncertainties. Therefore, it needs a comprehensive decision making model, which can improve the efficiency and effectiveness of health care service provision. Hospitals, as complex human service organizations, have highly interconnected and complex planning problems. This makes the development of decision making technology for planning and management a challenging task (McKee and Healy 2000).

Hospitals are one component of health service organizations. The resources involved, including humans, equipment, and infrastructures, are scarce and expensive. Hospitals consume great resources, and many of them tend to have low occupancy rates. Hospital managers face the task of utilizing existing resources more efficiently. Therefore, increasing the utilization of resources is a major managerial issue in hospital management. The need to use resources more cost-effectively has never been greater than it now is with diminishing resources and escalating costs. Hence, deploying resources with efficiency and effectiveness is a main target in hospital resource management (Marshall et al. 2002; Hutzschenreuter et al. 2009; Chawla and Govindaraj 1996).

There is much research into the resource management in primary work processes (direct patient treatment, such as surgery, intensive care, etc.) and secondary work

Q. Lin, *Analysis of Resource Management in Complex Work Systems*,
DOI 10.1007/978-981-10-2170-1_2

processes (supporting direct patient care, such as OR management, Laboratory diagnosis, etc.). However, there has been little research into resources in tertiary processes (supporting indirect patient care, such as sterile goods, etc.) (Marsolek and Friesdorf 2007). Sterile goods management is significant for primary work processes in hospitals. Sterile goods are operated in CSSD, which in most cases is located near the OT. Sterile processes incur high opportunity cost (Van de Klundert et al. 2008). Managing sterile goods and the use of valuable space (CSSD) near the OT for care and cure is important for hospital development. It involves decision making for sterile goods in hospitals.

2.2 Aims

Due to the complexity of resource management in the complex work system, especially in hospital complex systems, there is an urgent need to develop a scientific methodology to deal with the complexity and improve efficiency and effectiveness.

The main aim of this study is to develop and evaluate a conceptual framework of decision making models for resource management in highly complex work systems, using the example of sterile goods management in hospitals.

To accomplish this, the following sub-objectives are established:

- To outline the complexity of resource management in hospital using the example of sterile goods management
- To analyze the knowledge required for developing models
- To synthesize the knowledge in order to develop the following models
  - General Framework for complex work systems
  - Generic model for complex hospital systems
  - Specific model for outsourcing sterile goods decision in hospitals
- To evaluate the models.

In this study, the conceptual model is referred as DERESIS.

DEcision making model for ***RE***source Management of Complex Work ***S***ystem ***I***n ***S***terile Goods Management.

References

Chawla, M., & Govindaraj, R. (1996). Improving hospital performance through policies to increase hospital autonomy: Implementation guidelines. *Data for decision making project*. Retrieved November 22, 2012, from http://www.hsph.harvard.edu/ihsg/publications/pdf/No-32-1.PDF

Harper, P. R. (2002). A framework for operational modeling of hospital resources. *Health Care Management Science, 5*, 165–173.

Hutzschenreuter, A. K., Bosman, P. A. N., & Poutré, H. L. (2009). Evolutionary multiobjective optimization for dynamic hospital resource management. In A. Abraham, L. Jain, & R. Goldberg (Eds.), *Evolutionary multiobjective optimization*. Berlin, Heidelberg: Springer.

Marshall, A. H., Mcclean, S. I., Shapcott, C. M., & Millard, P. H. (2002). Modelling patient duration of stay to facilitate resource management of geriatric hospitals. *Health Care Management Science, 5*(4), 313–319.

Marsolek, I., & Friesdorf, W. (2007). Work systems and process analysis in health care. In P. Carayon (Ed.), *Handbook of human factors and ergonomics in health care and patient safety*. Mahwah, NJ: Lawrence Erlbaum Associates.

McKee, M., & Healy, J. (2000). The role of the hospital in a changing environment. *Bulletin of the World Health Organization, 78*(6), 803–810.

Van de Klundert, J., Muls, P., & Schadd, M. (2008). Optimizing sterilization logistics in hospitals. *Health Care Management Sci, 11*(1), 23–33.

Chapter 3
Methodical Approach

The methodological approach for the development of this methodology is based on the general problem-solving process in Systems Engineering.

Firstly, the situation analysis of resource management in complex work systems using the example of sterile goods management in hospital is presented. After the situation analysis, we formulate the objectives of the book: to develop the theoretical decision model for resource management in a complex work system. Then the synthesis and analysis concepts are considered by developing the DERESIS model, using a multidisciplinary approach. Lastly, the evaluation is investigated to clarify whether the developed model is suitable, and to what extent the model can be implemented realistically.

3.1 Foundation of the Methodology

The aim of this book is to develop a theoretical decision making model to provide guidance for the resource management in complex work systems. The methodology of "Systems Engineering (SE)" is used for this task. "*SE is a systematic way of thinking and a method to manage the problem solving processes in the context of challenging socio-technical questions. The application of SE is recommended for projects with large object complexity and large size where it is difficult to efficiently develop, implement and control a sustainable solution due to the many parties involved*" (Züst and Troxler 2006). It is a useful and efficient method for the realization of complex systems, and the objective is to structure and analyze complex problems successfully, to deduce systematic objectives and to find solutions, to make methodically supported decisions and to apply methods and techniques correctly and successfully (Schönsleben 2013). The problem solving cycle of SE involves several steps which are necessary to progress, in order to reach a solution (Züst 2004). These steps are situation analysis, objectives formulation, concept synthesis, concept analysis, evaluation, and decision making.

Q. Lin, *Analysis of Resource Management in Complex Work Systems*,
DOI 10.1007/978-981-10-2170-1_3

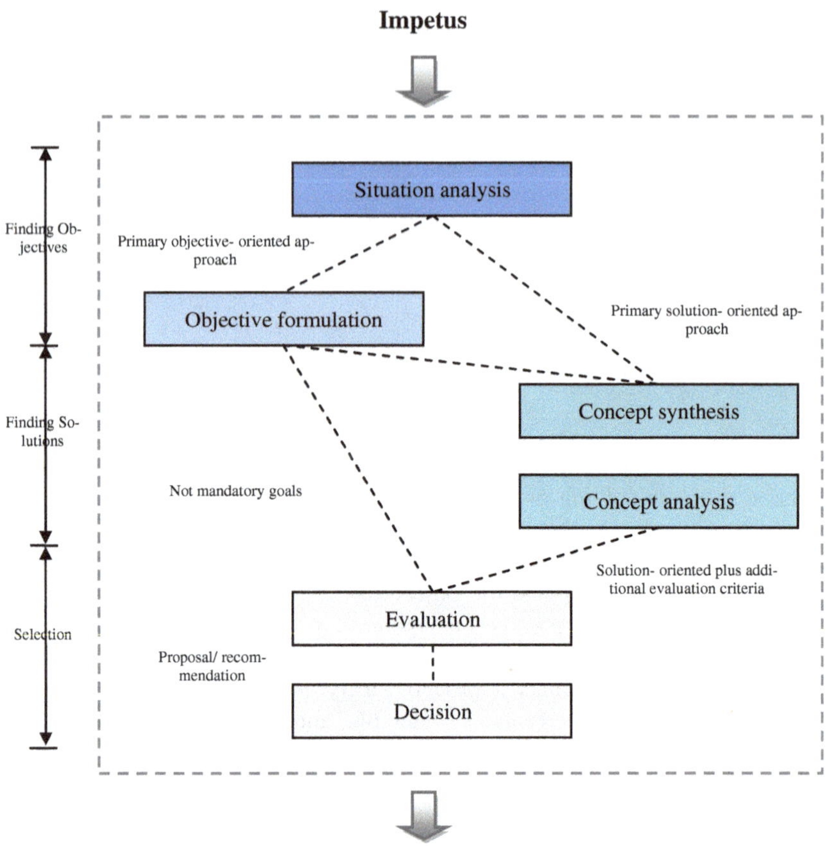

Fig. 3.1 The steps and the corresponding information flows of the problem solving cycle in systems engineering. *Source* Haberfellner et al. (1997)

Figure 3.1, which follows, illustrates the steps and the corresponding information flows of the problem solving cycle of SE.

3.2 Structure of the Book

This book is divided into three main parts: introduction (Chaps. 1–3), results (Chaps. 4–7) and the discussion and the prospect part (Chaps. 8 and 9). In the results part, the method of problem solving cycle of SE is used to develop the DERESIS model. Figure 3.2 illustrates the structure of the book.

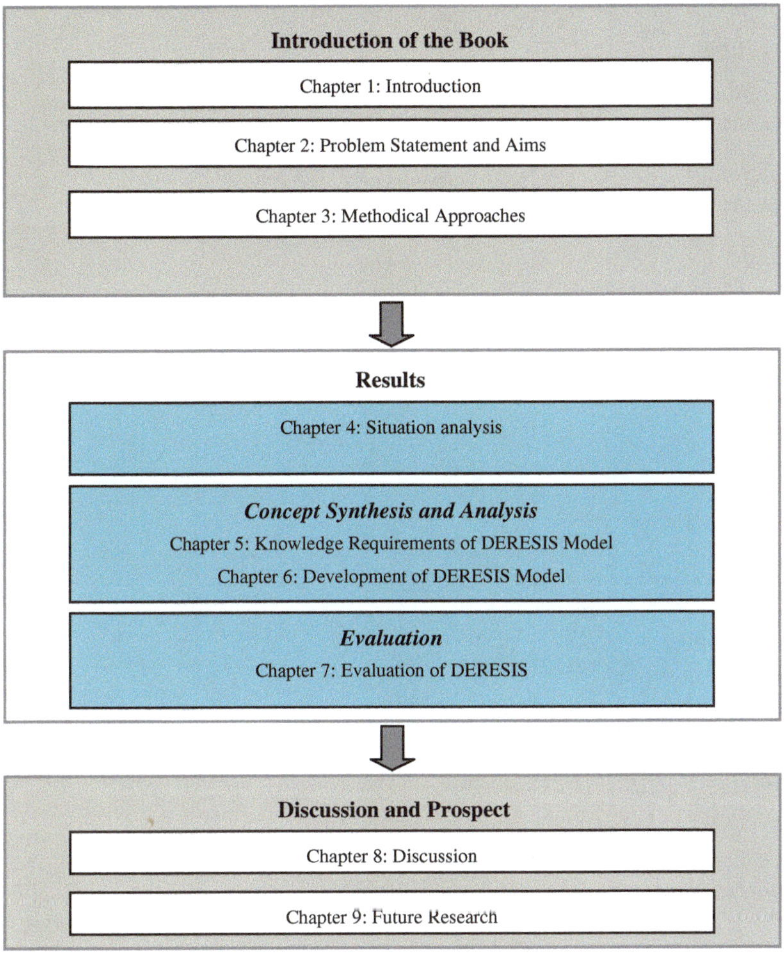

Fig. 3.2 The structure of the book

References

Haberfellner, R., Nagel, P., Becker, M., Büchel, A., & von Massow, H. (1997). *Systems engineering: Methodik und Praxis. 9. Verbesserte Auflage* (W. F. Daenzer, & F. Huber, Hrsg.). Zuerich: Verl. Industrielle Organisation.

Schönsleben, T. (2013). *Systems engineering methodology*. Retrieved May 24, 2013, from http://www.timgroup.ethz.ch/education/Courses_at_TIMGROUP/spring_2013/SE_FS_2013_final.pdf

Züst, R. (2004). *Einstieg ins systems engineering: Optimale, nachhaltige Lösungen, entwickeln und umsetzen*. Zürich: Verl. Industrielle Organisation.

Züst, R., & Troxler, P. (2006). *No more muddling through: Mastering complex projects in engineering and management*. Zürich: Orell Füssli Verlag.

Chapter 4
Situation of Resource Management

The four aspects of analysis of the situation of resource management are undertaken, using the example of sterile goods management in hospital, i.e. system-oriented analysis, cause-oriented analysis, future-oriented analysis, and solution-oriented analysis.

The system-oriented analysis starts with systems thinking to structure the situation of resource management, and to indicate the high relevance of the resources provision and treatment process. The cause-oriented analysis describes the sterile goods department as a kind of resource in hospital, its provision of sterile goods to the treatment process requires compatible cooperation. It reveals the networked influence of sterile goods provision. The future-oriented analysis shows that new strategies of resource provision can respond to the changing environment. Outsourcing is the most important issue when dealing with the challenges. The solution-oriented analysis presents solutions in order to make a sound decision about the resources in hospital.

4.1 System-Oriented Analysis

The health care system as a work system has been challenged in recent years to provide high quality service and solve complex problems but with limited resources. The effective delivery of resources is a fundamental aspect of health care management (Marshall et al. 2002). However, the provision of health care service is perhaps one of the most complex industries worldwide (Harper 2002). Providing appropriate medical care involves decision making in terms of planning and management of health care resources (Harper 2002). Administrators have to integrate the learned knowledge, experience, and information systems data to provide appropriate medical care and make correct decisions (Revere and Roberts 2004).

Q. Lin, *Analysis of Resource Management in Complex Work Systems*,
DOI 10.1007/978-981-10-2170-1_4

The Resource Management Initiative in the British National Health Service (NHS) was formally announced in 1986. The overriding aim of resource management was (Packwood et al. 1991):

> to enable the National Health Service to give a better service to its patients, by helping clinicians and other managers to make better informed judgments about how the resources they control can be used to the maximum effect

There are four key and inter-related elements contained within resource management: (1) improved quality of care; (2) involvement in management by the service providers; (3) improved information; (4) stronger control of resources (Packwood et al. 1991).

A hospital is one of the subsystems of the health care system. For years, hospitals have been forced by cost-saving pressures to improve their internal processes to ensure they remain competitive (Parsons et al. 1996). Hospital resource management is concerned with the efficient and effective deployment and allocation of resources, which include physical (e.g. buildings, equipment) and human (i.e. skills, capabilities, information and knowledge) resources. It deals with the way in which service providers, individually and collectively, plan, manage, deliver and evaluate services for patients. So successful resource management has to be sensitive and responsive to other demands and pressures (Packwood et al. 1991). In many hospitals, the resource management is a major managerial issue, due especially to the complex relationship between resources, utilization and patient throughput for different patient groups (Harper and Shahani 2002). Moreover, the problem is stochastic and dynamic as resource usage at a hospital unit behaves like a stochastic process and patient arrival and treatment processes are also stochastic. Different treatment processes for patients need to be considered. These typically involve several hospital units. And often, resources are shared by multiple treatment processes. Thus, hospital resource management is a complex and highly dynamic problem (Hutzschenreuter et al. 2009).

Central Sterile Supply Department (CSSD) is one of the physical resources in hospitals. It is sometimes known as a decontamination unit, and its role is to reprocess re-useable medical devices. It is a specialized area responsible for the collection, decontamination, assembling, packing, sterilization, storing and distribution of sterile goods and equipment to patient care areas (Lin et al. 2008). The supply of adequate sterile goods plays an essential role in the attempt to reduce the spreading of diseases within the health service (Ducel et al. 2002).

Sterile goods management in hospital is also a complex and highly dynamic problem. The hierarchical system structure is depicted in Fig. 4.1.

There is a need to analyze the interrelationship of different elements of work, when a health care system is viewed as a work system. Smith and Carayon (1989) and Carayon and Smith (2000) have developed the work system model, and characterized the many different elements of work: "*the individual performing different tasks with various tools and technologies in a physical environment under certain organizational conditions*". The health care system needs to adopt a systems approach to analysis, because of the different dimensions of system complexity

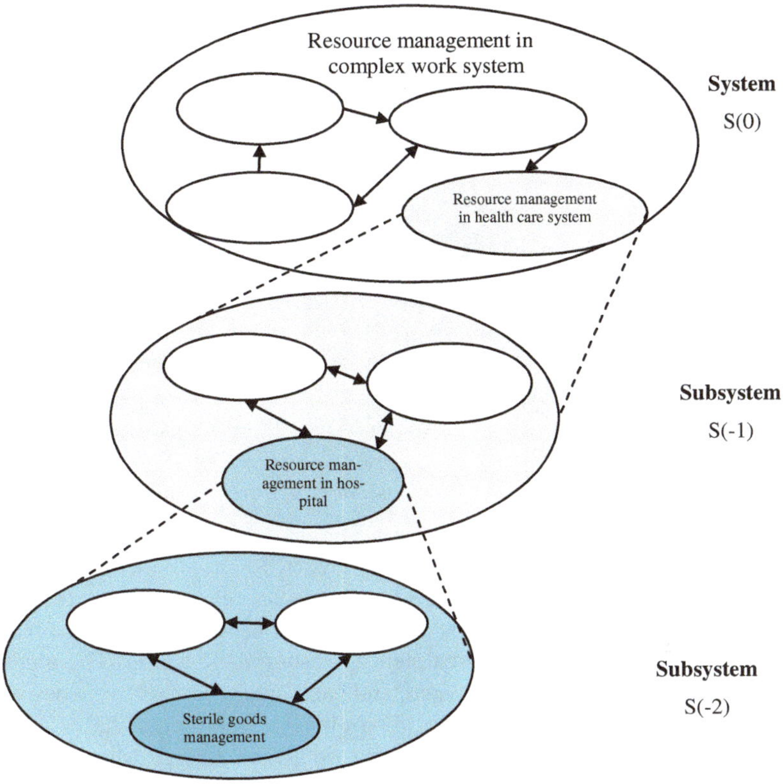

Fig. 4.1 The hierarchical system structure

(e.g. social aspects, dynamic character, many coupled subsystems, and uncertain data) (Vicente 1999, 2004). Friesdorf et al. (1990) proposed the Patient–Staff–Machine interaction model for health care systems. Patients, staff and machines are the core elements of health care work system. The interactions between the three elements represent the basis of the working processes that are essential to complete a given task objective (see Fig. 4.2).

The task objective of the patient–staff–machine health care system is defined by the staff according to the initial and the anticipated final patient status after task completion. If the task completion corresponds to the task objective, the quality is high. High quality can be achieved only if the working processes are performed correctly. Efficiency must take the used resources into account (Carayon and Friesdorf 2006). High efficiency requires high quality and with fewer resources. Therefore, resource management is important for the efficiency of the health care work system. Resources are also a very important aspect in order to guarantee the work processes in health care work systems.

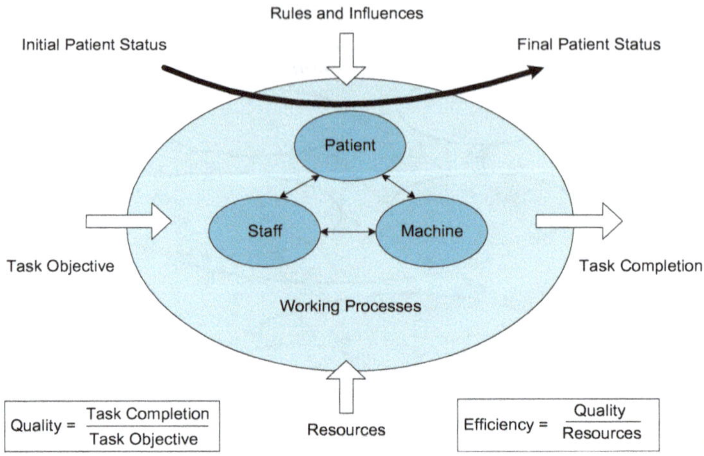

Fig. 4.2 Medical work processes and their context in a work system. *Source* Carayon and Friesdorf (2006)

Patient treatment in a high dependency environment is a very complex and dynamic process (Marsolek and Friesdorf 2007). Friesdorf et al. (2011) proposed the 6-layer model to link patient treatment to resource allocation. The model differentiates six layers of patient treatment, and each layer contains two sides: the left side reflects the treatment processes; the right side represents the provision of resources. Both sides are linked by bridges on which Bridge Managers (BrMs) coordinate and control the resource allocation to the needs of patient treatment processes (see Appendix 1). On each layer the BrMs must plan, allocate and assign the required resource for the needs of the treatment processes. How to provide the required resource to support the treatment processes is the main task of resource management. This involves making resource decisions.

4.2 Cause-Oriented Analysis

There are three different types of work processes within medical work (Friesdorf et al. 2002; Marsolek and Friesdorf 2007):

- Primary work processes: the direct patient treatment processes (e.g. a surgical intervention, an intensive care treatment).
- Secondary work processes: Processes directly supporting the patient treatment processes (e.g. the OR management, laboratory diagnostics).
- Tertiary work processes: Processes indirectly supporting the patient treatment processes (e.g., sterilization, cleaning, catering).

The sterilization process belongs to the tertiary work processes within medical work. Marsolek and Friesdorf (2007) has concluded that "*Secondary and tertiary work processes have a rather low level of complexity compared to primary work processes. Traditional analysis and optimization strategies for classical work systems can be applied*". However, sterile goods are needed in all three types of work processes. Therefore, sterile goods management is complex and must be based on the analysis of all three types of processes, and the analysis of the logistics of sterile goods within the different work processes. Cost reductions in sterile goods management will free up money for the improvement of primary processes directly related to the cure and care of patients (Van de Klundert et al. 2008).

The main purpose of sterile goods management is to provide sterilized equipment to hospital theatres and other departments. Sterile goods management is carried out in CSSD. CSSD is the backbone of hospital functions. It comprises the service within the hospital in which medical/surgical supplies and equipment, both sterilized and non-sterilized, are cleaned, prepared, processed, packed, stored, and issued for patient care (SMPD 2013). It receives stores, sterilizes and distributes them to many areas including the wards, outpatient departments and other special units such as operating theatres (OT) (Allison 1960).

OT is typically the CSSD's largest and most demanding customer. The instruments and sets, which are sterilized and are delivered on time, are important for perioperative patients. CSSD services the OT directly, but the patients indirectly (Barlow 2010). However, OT is the important location for surgical intervention, which is the direct patient treatment process. So cooperation between the CSSD and OT affects patient safety, and the success of surgical procedures. The Association of Perioperative Registerer of Nurses (AORN'S) Position Statement on Patient Safety states (Seavey 2007):

> The safety of patients undergoing operative or other invasive procedures is a primary responsibility of the perioperative registered nurse. Registered nurses form a professional bond with patients, who place their physical and emotional well-being in the hands of registered nurses and their surgical colleagues and who believe that the care provided will be safe and effective. The patient/caregiver bond is founded on the patient's trust in the registered nurse and the surgical team. Protecting the patient and promoting an optimal surgical outcome further strengthens that bond.

Here the "surgical colleagues" and "surgical team" include the instrument reprocessing staff. They are a part of the surgical team, and should be held accountable for patient safety along with the registered nurse, the surgeon, the anaesthetist and the scrub technologist. Therefore, in order to improve patient safety, CSSD and OT must work together harmoniously (Seavey 2007). A compatible relationship between the two departments must rely on constructive and determined efforts, such as caring, cooperation, collaboration, and networking. Currently, there has been much research into the connection between the CSSD and OT (King 2009; Gallousis 1990; Friedman 1990; Seavey 2010; Stewart 2011). A rudimentary design for sterile logistics is presented in Fig. 4.3. The layout of CSSD and the general flow of sterile goods between OR and CSSD are described in Appendix 2 and Appendix 3.

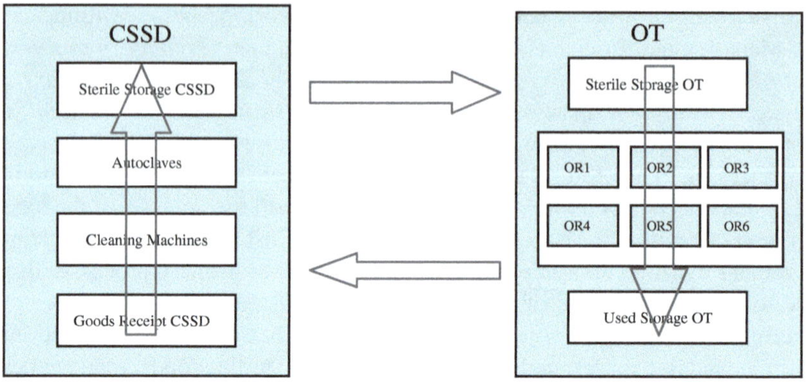

Fig. 4.3 Rudimentary design for sterile logistics. *Source* Van de Klundert et al. (2008)

CSSD must provide the correct instrument packages required to the correct ORs at the correct time to support the surgical schedule in OR. For large OT suites, CSSD management is challenging, because of the inconsistent arrival of dirty instruments. Trays of dirty instruments do not arrive at a constant rate, but arrive in bursts which coincide with the completion of surgery. This can result in significant accumulations of instruments at different points in the sterilization process, and this would complicate staff scheduling and equipment capacity specifications (Lin et al. 2008).

Attention for optimizing the logistic processes involved in sterile goods logistics has increased, centered on the CSSD and OT. In particular, there is much attention for outsourcing of the CSSD. But there are few discussions in scientific literature about how to make the decisions for hospital managers about outsourcing and in-house, which will improve hospital development.

Moreover, CSSD is located near the OT, in a central position in the hospital. Using this important space for care and cure, rather than for the secondary sterilization processes, should provide opportunities to improve the service to patients. Moreover, CSSD is capital intensive, and employs thousands of people. Whether it is via taxes or via insurance payments, the expense that comes with the required availability of sterile instruments is paid for by the customer, i.e. the patient (Van de Klundert et al. 2008). Therefore, the management of sterile goods is important for patients and hospital development.

4.3 Future-Oriented Analysis

With an ageing population and the rise in health care spending, hospitals and other health care organizations face unparalleled pressures to change in the future. They must address a variety of challenges to provide more services and better quality with few extra financial, material, and human resources. Health care organizations have to ensure efficiency in resource allocation, and develop an innovative health care system that is better capable of responding to patient expectations, as well as enabling high quality service delivery (Clough 2011; Syed 2005; Akdag 2010).

With changes occurring everywhere, hospital managers have to development new strategies in order to adapt to rapidly changing conditions. In order to survive in a competitive market and to accomplish long term growth, hospitals are taking steps to focus their business on their core competency, i.e. the delivery of health care services, to improve efficiency and reduce costs. In addition, more and more hospitals are exploring outsourcing as a way to deal with these challenges (Lyles et al. 2010; HFMA 2012). Outsourcing of health services is a controversial issue presently, and will be in the future. It is increasingly seen as a policy tool with the potential to increase the quality and efficiency of health care (Albreht 2009; Karimi et al. 2012; Laamanen et al. 2008).

Outsourcing is "*any task, operation, job or process that could be performed by employees within a company, but is instead contracted to a third party for significant period of time*" (Bucki 2013). Outsourcing allows health care organizations to reduce costs, increase efficiency and service quality, bring staff and patient satisfaction, introduce labor market flexibility, and focus on core competencies. Organizations focus on core competencies which provide high value, maximize return on internal resources, and they treat many services as strategic enablers (Young 2005; Moschuris and Kondylis 2006; Ferdosi et al. 2013; Lyles et al. 2010).

Health care organizations have continued to outsource a multitude of non-core services. The most common outsourced tasks include: revenue cycle services, human resources, benefits administration, information technology, laundry, housekeeping, food services (Lyles et al. 2010; HFMA 2012; Karimi et al. 2012; Lin et al. 2010). When managed care programs attempt to reduce health care cost, providers are turning to outsourcing in new ways, in order to endeavor to maintain high standards of care whilst addressing current economic realities. Health care organizations are considering outsourcing as a possible response to demands created by such factors as market pressures, requirements of managed care organizations, mergers and acquisitions, and competition within the industry (Moschuris and Kondylis 2006).

There are so many reasons for outsourcing in hospitals; the main ones are: reducing costs and increasing efficiency; gaining competitive advantage; access to key technologies; reducing and sharing risk; access to capital resources; workforce flexibility; focusing on goals (Ferdosi et al. 2013; Young 2005; Karimi et al. 2012).

The main objective of outsourcing is that it allows a health care organization to concentrate on its core processes and its customers. It results in greater efficiency and quality of services (Akdag 2010). The benefits of the outsourcing in health care organizations can be listed as follows (see Table 4.1) (Akdag 2010; Kremic et al. 2006).

The outsourced services provide more sophisticated technology, an increase in in-house capacity and a saving in capital expenditure. Outsourcing has grown rapidly in health care, and it has been extended to administrative services and core

Table 4.1 Benefits of outsourcing

	Benefits of outsourcing
1	Reduces overhead expenses, frees up resources
2	Minimizes capital expenditures
3	Eliminates investments in fixed infrastructure
4	Offloads non-core functions
5	Redirects energy and personnel into the core business
6	Frees the executive team from problems of daily routine processes
7	Focuses scarce resources on mission-oriented projects
8	Ensures access to specialized skills
9	Saves on manpower and training costs
10	Controls operating costs
11	Makes the economics of scale available by enhancing efficiency
12	Improves speed and service
13	Eliminates peak staffing problems
14	Provides the best quality services, products and people
15	Is reliable and innovative
16	Provides value-added services
17	Increases customer satisfaction
18	Establishes long-term strategic relationships with world-class service providers to gain a competitive edge
19	Enhances tactical and strategic advantages
20	Enables strategic thinking, process reengineering and managing relationships with trade partners
21	Benefits from the provider's expertise in solving problems for a variety of clients with similar requirements.

services (Akdag 2010). Nevertheless, the outsourcing will also increase scheduling problems, quality control problems, and increase dependency. Therefore, although outsourcing may provide major benefits in terms of sharing expensive equipment and providing extra capacity, there is a danger that such outsourcing may in itself result in increased uncertainty and quality problems (Savage 1996; Prahalad and Hamel 1994; Renner and Palmer 1999).

4.4 Solution-Oriented Analysis

Facing pressure to reduce costs and improve the efficiency and effectiveness of resource utilization, outsourcing a multitude of noncore and core services, is a growing trend in hospital management (Lyles et al. 2010; HFMA 2012; Akdag 2010). The strategy to implement outsourcing would have a significant impact on its effectiveness. However, outsourcing would increase scheduling problems and uncertainty. It could also have a negative effect on the quality of patient care

(Savage 1996; Prahalad and Hamel 1994; Renner and Palmer 1999; Ferdosi et al. 2013; Lethbridge 2012). Therefore, the decision as to whether or not to outsource is important for hospital development. The solution lies in making a sound decision about the outsourcing of resources in hospital.

Decision making about outsourcing in a hospital is difficult, comprehensive, and complex. The factors, which may impact the outsourcing decision, would be the expected benefits, potential risks, strategy, cost, function characteristics, and environmental concerns (Kremic et al. 2006). It is difficult and complex for hospital managers to obtain and assess all the factors, in order to make a sound decision. Techniques and scientific methods are required to make well-informed decisions about the trade-off between costs and quality (Mangroelal 2010; Dibbern et al. 2004).

Over recent decades, a number of approaches have been developed to analyze decisions, including evidence-based analysis, cost-effectiveness analysis, and equity analysis. However, these approaches concentrate only on single criteria, whereas in reality, particularly in complex working systems, decision makers need to make choices considering multiple criteria simultaneously, both quantitative and qualitative (Baltussen and Niessen 2006; Brownson et al. 1999; Altrock and Krause 1994; Hong and Choi 2000).

4.4.1 Decision Making

What is decision making? Harris describes it as:

> Decision making is the study of identifying and choosing alternatives based on the values and preferences of the decision makers. It is the process of sufficiently reducing uncertainty and doubt about alternatives to allow a reasonable choice to be made from among them (Harris 2012).

Decision making is often viewed as a stage of processing human information. In order to make decisions, people must gather, organize, and combine information from various sources. Information processing has become a part of decision making, as decisions become more complex (Lehto and Nah 2006).

Making decisions in complex domains, such as in health care systems, can be considered to be a function of the decision task itself, as well as the expertise of the decision maker (Kushniruk 2001). Decision makers continually face the difficult task of balancing benefits against costs, and the risks of realizing the benefits (Phillips and Bana e Costa 2005). Making decisions is often complicated in health care, because of ambiguity of information, differing interpretations of the evidence, and the differing perspectives and backgrounds of decision makers (Kushniruk 2001).

Decision Making Process

Managers in organizations make a wide variety of decisions, due to the complexity and diversity of management activities. Managerial decisions are classified as: strategic decisions, tactical decisions, and operation decisions (Fountas et al. 2006). No matter which type of decision is made, it is necessary to analyze the decision making process.

Decision making is a process which decision makers use to reach a decision. The core of this process is described by Simon in three phases: intelligence, design, and choice (Jawadekar 2007; Simon 1960). The intelligence phase relates to the identification of the problem which needs to be solved. It consists of finding, identifying, and formulating the problem or situation which calls for a decision to be made. The design phase refers to alternative solutions, developing and analyzing them. The choice phase consists of using the selection criteria to choose from the various alternative solutions (Dibbern et al. 2004; Jawadekar 2007). The decision making process, based on this concept, is depicted in Fig. 4.4.

The three phases are not linear, but often cyclical and result in a single decision being made (see Fig. 4.5) (Wickens et al. 2004).

The cycle of phases is far more complex. Each phase of the process is itself a complex decision making process. The design phase may call for new intelligence activities. Problems at any given level generate sub-problems (Simon 1960).

Using Simon's decision making model, there are some researchers who propose the following decision making processes: the six steps decision making process (Kartha 2012; Foster 2010), the eight steps decision making process (Baker et al. 2001), etc. Simon's model is a general model for decision making, but it needs to be adapted when analyzing the specific decision making (Dibbern et al. 2004).

The decision making process is a complex process in the higher hierarchy of management. This is because of factors such as inter-relationship between the decision makers, job responsibilities, and question of feasibility, the moral and ethical code and the probable impact on business (Jawadekar 2007).

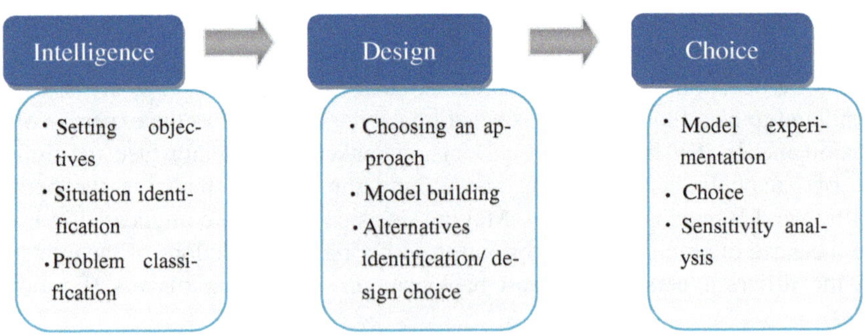

Fig. 4.4 Decision making process. *Source* Seok et al. (2012)

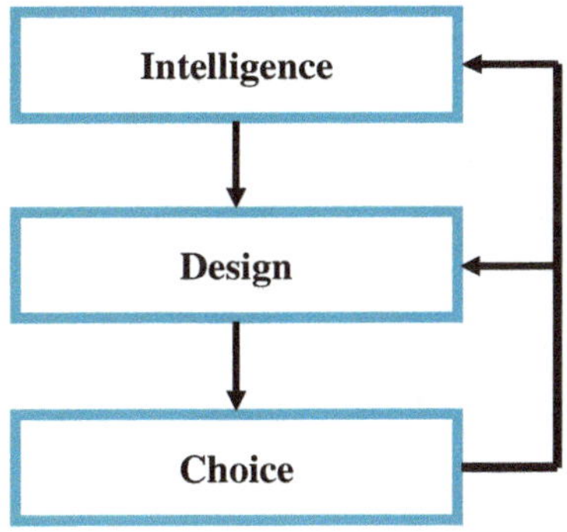

Fig. 4.5 Herbert Simon decision making model. *Source* Jawadekar (2007)

Appendix 1: The 6-Layer Model

The 6-layer model links patient treatment to resource allocation (Friesdorf et al. 2011, p. 417). It is developed to improve patient treatment by planning and managing treatment processes and controlling resources (Fuchs 2013, p. 139). The model differentiates six layers of patient treatment, and each layer contains two sides: the left side represents the treatment processes, and the right side the provision of resources. Both sides are linked by bridges by which Bridge Managers (BrMs) coordinate and control the resource allocation to the needs of patient treatment processes (Hoge et al. 2012, p. 149).

Layer 1: Cases: Classification by case groups considering the overall treatment of an individual patient (for example DRGs in Germany etc.).
Layer 2: Stages: Sequences of treatments by different sectors (general practitioner, ambulance, hospital, rehabilitation). The linearity of the treatment process is resolved by the decision models—such as outpatient or inpatient care.
Layer 3: Stations: Components of the treatment in different organizational units within one structure, e.g. in hospital: emergency room, operating room, intensive care unit.
Layer 4: Phases: Sub-tasks within a station—the sequence of treatments of the patient in a particular "Station"
Layer 5: Modules: Structuring a treatment "Phase" into diagnosis and patient-specific bundles of individual medical interventions, such as cardiovascular treatment of heart failure
Layer 6: Arrangements: All individual medical measures, such as administration of an analog sedation, blood pressure measurement (Fuchs 2013, pp. 71, 143; Friesdorf et al. 2011, p. 420). The 6-layer model is shown in Fig. 4.6.

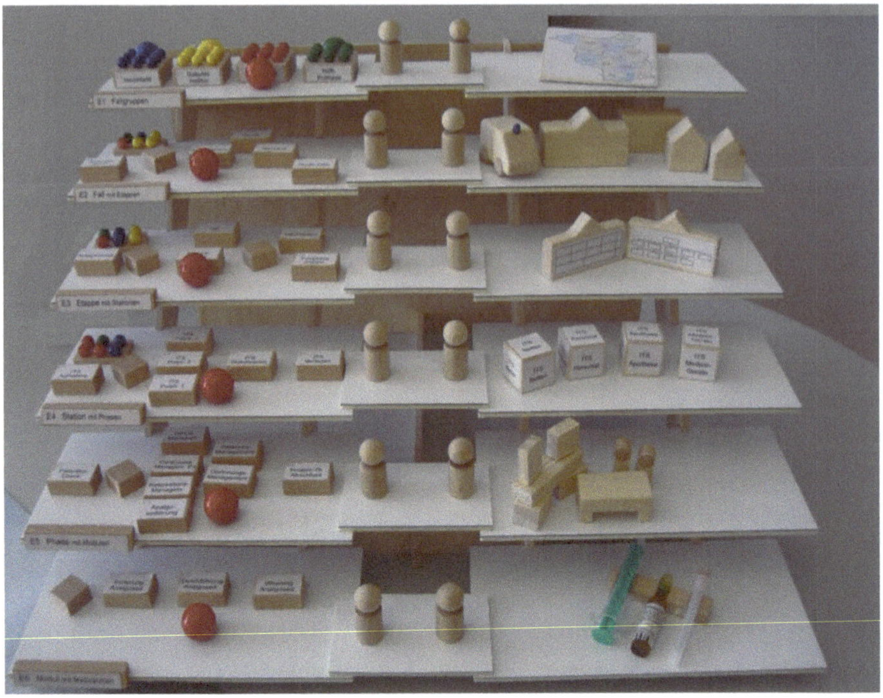

Fig. 4.6 The 6-layer model

Appendix 2: The Layout of CSSD

See Fig. 4.7.

Fig. 4.7 The layout of CSSD

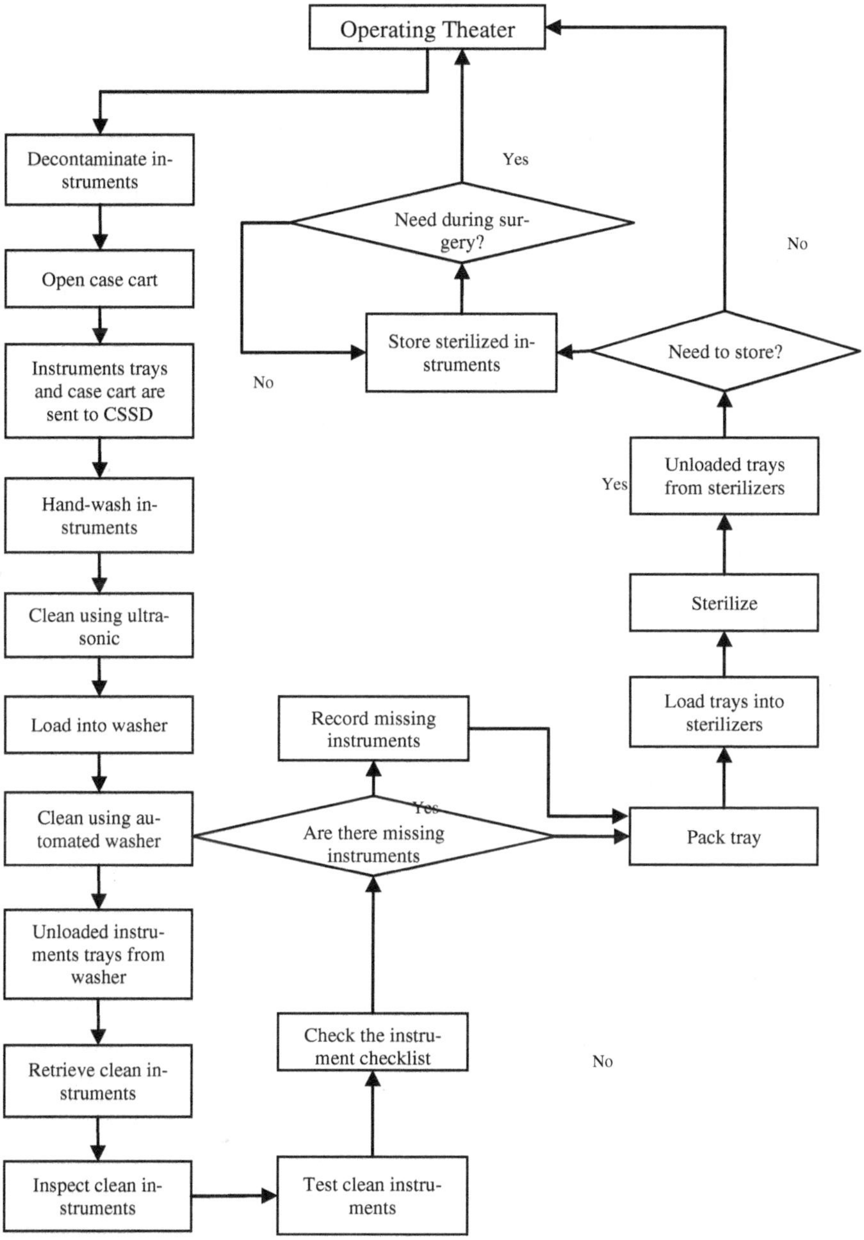

Fig. 4.8 The general flow of instruments between OT and CSSD

Appendix 3: The General Flow of Sterile Goods Between Operating Theatre and Central Sterile Supply Department

Sterile goods are always stocked. They are not stocked individually, but grouped in nets. One net includes all the items needed for a particular surgery. However, in general, the net more commonly applies to several types of surgery, and one type of surgery requires nets of a distinct type. Before an operation, the required nets are taken from the sterile storage CSSD, and will be taken to the appropriate OR. During the operation, the sterile items, whether they are used or not, will become contaminated. After surgery, all items will be brought to the contaminated storage facility of the OT, from where they will be taken to the goods reception of CSSD. There they are pre-cleaned, and then put into the washing machines. After washing, the materials are reassembled and regrouped to form nets. The nets are put into the autoclaves where the sterilization takes place. After sterilization, the nets are placed in the sterile storage of CSSD. From there they are brought to the sterile storage of OT. This completes the closed loop (Van de Klundert et al. 2008, p. 24; Lin et al. 2008, p. 558). Figure 4.8 provides the general flow of the instruments between OT and CSSD.

References

Akdag, R. (2010). *Outsourcing practices in the Turkish health care system: Survey report*. Ankara: School of Public Health. Retrieved March 10, 2013, from http://ekutuphane.tusak.gov.tr/kitaplar/outsourcing_practices_in_the_turkish_health_care_system.pdf

Albreht, T. (2009). Privatization processes in health care in Europe—A move in the right direction, a trendy option, or a step back. *European Journal of Public Health, 19*(5), 448–451.

Allison, V. D. (1960). Hospital central sterile supply departments. *Medical Journal, 2*, 772–778.

Altrock, C. V., & Krause, B. (1994). Multi-criteria decision making in German automotive industry using fuzzy logic. *Fuzzy Sets and Systems, 63*(3), 375–380.

Baker, D., Bridges, D., Hunter, R., Johnson, G., Krupa, J., Murphy, J., et al. (2001). *Guidebook to decision making methods*. Retrieved January 11, 2013, from http://kscsma.ksc.nasa.gov/Reliability/Documents/Decision_Making_Guidebook_2002_Dept_of_Energy.phd

Baltussen, R., & Niessen, L. (2006). Priority setting of health interventions: The need for multi-criteria decision analysis. *Cost Effectiveness and Resource Allocation, 4*(14), 1–9.

Barlow, R. D. (2010). Heart of the hospital. *Healthcare Purchasing News, 5*, 10–14.

Brownson, R. C., Gurney, J. G., & Land, G. H. (1999). Evidence-based decision making in public health. *Journal Public Health Management Practice, 5*(5), 86–97.

Bucki, J. (2013). *Introduction of outsourcing*. Retrieved December 15, 2012, from http://operationstech.about.com/od/costsavingstrategies/a/OutSrcDefine.htm

Carayon, P., & Friesdorf, W. (2006). Human factors and ergonomics in medicine. In G. Salvendy (Ed.), *Handbook of human factors and ergonomics*. New Jersey: Wiley.

Carayon, P., & Smith, M. J. (2000). Work organization and ergonomics. *Applied Ergonomics, 31*, 649–662.

Clough, J. (2011). *Committee on performance improvement: Hospitals and care systems of the future*. Chicago: American Hospital Association. Retrieved January 25, 2013, from http://www.aha.org/content/11/hospitals-care-systems-of-future.pdf

Dibbern, J., Goles, T., Hirschheim, R., & Jayatilaka, B. (2004). Information system outsourcing: A survey and analysis of the literature. *ACM SIGMIS Database, 35*(4), 6–102.

Ducel, G., Fabry, J., & Nicolle, L. (2002). *Prevention of hospital—Acquired infections*, 2nd ed. World Healthcare Organization. Retrieved January 20, 2013, from http://www.who.int/csr/resources/publications/whocdscsreph200212.pdf

Ferdosi, M., Farahabadi, E., Mofid, M., Rejalian, F., Haqhiqhat, M., & Naquhdi, P. (2013). Evaluation of outsourcing in nursing services: A case study of Kashani hospitals, Isfahan in 2011. *Mater Sociomed, 25*(1), 37–39.

Foster, D. (2010). *6 steps to better decision making*. Retrieved February 10, 2013, from http://www.coachdanfoster.com/2010/05/6-steps-to-better-decision-making/

Fountas, S., Wulfsohn, D., Blackmore, B. S., Jacobsen, H. L., & Pedersen, S. M. (2006). A model of decision-making and information flows for information-intensive agriculture. *Agricultural System, 87*, 192–210.

Friedman, B. B. (1990). The four Cs of a successful central sterile supply—Operating room relationship. *Hospital Materiel Management Quarterly, 12*(2), 26–31.

Friesdorf, W., Marsolek, I., & Goebel, M. (2002). Integrative concepts for the OR. *Journal of Clinical Monitoring and Computing, 17*(7–8), 489–490.

Friesdorf, W., Mendyk, S., Sander, H., & Podtschaske, B. (2011). Arbeitssystem Gesundheitswesen – eine Herausforderung für die Arbeitswissenschaft. In: B. Spanner-Ulmer (Hrsg.). *Mensch, Technik, Organisation – Vernetzung im Produktentstehungs- und Herstellungsprozess. 57. Frühjahrskongress der Gesellschaft für Arbeitswissenschaft* (pp. 417–420). Technische Universität Chemnitz, März 23–25, 2001. Dortmund: GfA Press.

Friesdorf, W., Schwilk, B., Hahnel, J., Fett, P., & Weideck, H. (1990). Ergonomics applied to an intensive care workplace. *Intensive Care World, 7*(4), 192–198.

Fuchs, D. (2013). *Entwicklung eines Vorgehensmodells zur Prozessorientierten Plannung und Gestaltung komplexer Arbeitssysteme (Am Beispiel Krankenhaus)*. Berlin: Technischen Universität Berlin, der Fakultät VII – Wirschaft und Management.

Gallousis, A. J. (1990). The central sterile supply—Operating room connection. *Hospital Materiel Management Quarterly, 12*(2), 20–22.

Harper, P. R. (2002). A framework for operational modeling of hospital resources. *Health Care Management Science, 5*, 165–173.

Harper, P. R., & Shahani, A. K. (2002). Modelling for the planning and management of bed capacities in hospitals. *Journal of the Operational Research Society, 53*, 11–18.

Harris, R. (2012). *Introduction to decision making*. Retrieved December 10, 2012, from http://www.virtualsalt.com/crebook5.htm.

HFMA. (2012). *Using outsourcing to transform human resource functions. Educational report.* Retrieved January 21, 2013, from: http://www.adp.com/tools-and-resources/industry-vertical-markets/~/media/AC9DE651F154448FB757276F9F4255A2.ashx

Hoge, Y. G., Fuchs, D., Koller, W., & Friesdorf, W. (2012). Supporting structures for information transfer in ICUs. In V. G. Duffy (Ed.), *Advances in human aspects of healthcare*. Boca Raton: Taylor & Francis Group.

Hong, D. H., & Choi, C. H. (2000). Multicriteria fuzzy decision-making problems based on vague set theory. *Fuzzy Sets and Systems, 114*(1), 103–113.

Hutzschenreuter, A. K., Bosman, P. A. N., & Poutré, H. L. (2009). Evolutionary multiobjective optimization for dynamic hospital resource management. In A. Abraham, L. Jain, & R. Goldberg (Eds.), *Evolutionary multiobjective optimization*. Berlin, Heidelberg: Springer.

Jawadekar, W. S. (2007). *Management information systems: Texts and cases* (3rd ed.). New Delhi: Tata McGraw-Hill Publishing.

Karimi, S., Agharahimi, Z., & Yaghoubi, M. (2012). Impacts of outsourcing in educational hospitals in Iran: A study on Isfahan University of Medical Sciences-2010. *Journal of Education and Health Promotion, 1*(25), 1–5. Retrieved January 10, 2013, from http://www.jehp.net/temp/JEduHealthPromot1125-1729484_044814.pdf

Kartha, D. (2012). *6 steps to decision-making process*. Retrieved February 15, 2013, from http://www.buzzle.com/articles/6-steps-to-decision-making-process.html

King, C. M. (2009). Survive and thrive: Guide for new SPD managers. *Healthcare Purchasing News*, May, 24–26. Retrieved March 3, 2013, from http://www.hpnonline.com/ce/pdfs/0905cetest.pdf

Kremic, T., Tukel, O. I., & Rom, W. O. (2006). Outsourcing decision support: A survey of benefits, risks, and decision factors. *Supply Chain Management: An International Journal, 11*(6), 467–482.

Kushniruk, A. W. (2001). Analysis of complex decision-making processes in health care: Cognitive approaches to health informatics. *Journal of Biomedical Informatics, 34*, 365–376.

Laamanen, R., Simonsen-Rehn, N., Suominen, S., Φvretveit, J., & Brommels, M. (2008). Outsourcing primary health care services—How politicians explain the grounds for their decisions. *Health Policy, 88*, 294–307.

Lehto, M. R., & Nah, F. (2006). Decision-making model and decision support. In G. Salvendy (Ed.), *Handbook of human factors and ergonomics* (3rd ed.). New York: Wiley.

Lethbridge, J. (2012). *Empty promises: The impact of outsourcing on NHS services*. Technical report. Retrieved December 25, 2012, from http://www.psiru.org/sites/default/files/2012-04-H%20UNISONEmptyPromisesOutsourcing_0.pdf

Lin, C., Huang, Y. A., Li, C. F., & Jalleh, G. (2010). Key health information system outsourcing issues from six hospital cases. In M. S. Al-Mutairi & L. A. Mohammed (Eds.), *Cases on ICT utilization, practice and solutions: Tools for managing day-to-day issues*. Pennsylvania: IGI Global.

Lin, F., Lawley, M., Spry, C., Mccarthy, K., Coyle-Rogers, P. G., & Yih, Y. (2008). Using simulation to design a central sterilization department. *AORN Journal, 88*(4), 555–567.

Lyles, K. D., Helms, S. C., & Lykins, A. (2010). Healthcare outsourcing overview: Staying focused in uncertain times. *A Publication of the American Health Lawyers Association Teaching Hospitals & Academic Medical Centers Practicfe Group, 7*(1), 1–5. Retrieved January 21, 2013, from http://www.jonesday.com/files/Publication/03293b67-5563-48a6-97f4-fb157db2d369/Presentation/PublicationAttachment/c91e37d5-93de-476f-94c3-42bfcac58e92/Lyles_Helms_Lykins%20article.pdf

Mangroelal, N. D. (2010). *IT-outsourcing in hospitals: Towards an outsourcing model for decision support*. Master Business Informatics. Retrieved January 5, 2013, from https://www.google.de/url?sa=t&rct=j&q=&esrc=s&source=web&cd=1&cad=rja&ved=0CDUQFjAA&url=http%3A%2F%2Fwww.cs.uu.nl%2Feducation%2Fscripties%2Fpdf.php%3FSID%3DINF%2FSCR-2009-087&ei=yJ4-UoGAMamH0AWT54HQBw&usg=AFQjCNEdsIW4X7wuy4JAiYzLqk6qX-i2oA&sig2=YJHRIXeOEnX0Ac3osAJZ-Q&bvm=bv.52434380,d.Yms

Marshall, A. H., Mcclean, S. I., Shapcott, C. M., & Millard, P. H. (2002). Modelling patient duration of stay to facilitate resource management of geriatric hospitals. *Health Care Management Science, 5*(4), 313–319.

Marsolek, I., & Friesdorf, W. (2007). Work systems and process analysis in health care. In P. Carayon (Ed.), *Handbook of human factors and ergonomics in health care and patient safety*. Mahwah, NJ: Lawrence Erlbaum Associates.

Moschuris, S. J., & Kondylis, M. N. (2006). Outsourcing in public hospitals: A greek perspective. *Journal of Health Organization and Management, 20*(1), 4–14.

Packwood, T., Keen, J., & Buxton, M. (1991). *Hospitals in transition: The resource management experiment*. Bristol: Open University Press.

Parsons, M. L., Murdaugh, C. L., Purdon, T. F., & Jarrell, B. E. (1996). *Guide to clinical resource management*. Gaithersburg: Aspen Publishers.

Phillips, L. D., & Bana e Costa, C. A. (2005). *Transparent prioritization, budgeting and resource allocation with multi-criteria decision analysis and decision conferencing*. Working Paper. Retrieved February 13, 2012, from http://eprints.lse.ac.uk/22742/1/05075.phd

Prahalad, C. K., & Hamel, G. (1994). Strategy as a field of study: Why search for a new paradigm? *Strategic Management Journal, 15*(S2), 5–16.

Renner, C., & Palmer, E. (1999). Outsourcing to increase service capacity in a New Zealand hospital. *Journal of Management in Medicine, 13*(5), 325–338.

Revere, L., & Roberts, R. (2004). Improving resource efficiency through management science. *Journal of Healthcare Management, 49*(5), 323–335.

Savage, T. (1996). Inside outsourcing. *Hospital and Health Networks, 70*(20), 44–45.

Seavey, R. (2007). OR and SPD working together to improve instrument processing. *Education & Training*, July, 84–102. Retrieved March 2, 2013, from http://www.csao.net/files/pdfs/OR%20and%20SPD%20Working%20Together707.pdf

Seavey, R. E. (2010). Collaboration between perioperative nurses and sterile processing department personnel. *AORN Journal, 91*(4), 454–462.

Seok, H. S., Nof, S. Y., & Filip, F. G. (2012). Sustainability decision support system based on collaborative control theory. *Annual Reviews in Control, 36*(1), 85–100.

Simon, H. A. (1960). *The new science of management decision*. New York: Harper & Brothers Publishers.

Smith, M. J., & Carayon, P. (1989). A balanced theory of job design for stress reduction. *International Journal of Industrial Ergonomics, 4*, 67–79.

SMPD. (2013). *Basics on processing & sterilization*. In: University of Rochester Medical Center. Retrieved March 14, 2013, from http://www.urmc.rochester.edu/sterile/basics.cfm

Stewart, S. (2011). Tearing down the Wallls between OR and SPD. *Canadian Operating Room Nursing Journal*. Retrieved January 20, 2013, from http://findarticles.com/p/articles/mi_qa4130/is_200406/ai_n9465283/

Syed, S. (2005). *Resource utilization: How hospitalists add value to the bottom line*. Retrieved March 20, 2013, from http://www.the-hospitalist.org/details/article/257875/Resource_Utilization_How_Hospitalists_Add_Value_to_the_Bottom_Line.html

Van de Klundert, J., Muls, P., & Schadd, M. (2008). Optimizing sterilization logistics in hospitals. *Health Care Management Science, 11*(1), 23–33.

Vicente, K. J. (1999). *Cognitive work analysis: Toward safe, productive, and healthy comuper-based work*. Mahwah, NJ: Lawrence Erlbaum Associates.

Vincent, C. A. (2004). Analysis of clinical incidents: A window on the system not a search for root causes. *Quality and Safety in Health Care, 13*, 242–243.

Wickens, C. D., Lee, J., Liu, Y. L., & Becker, S. G. (2004). *An introduction to human factors engineering* (2nd ed.). New Jersey: Pearson Education.

Young, S. (2005). Outsourcing in the Australian health sector: The interplay of economics and politics. *International Journal of Public Sector Management, 18*(1), 25–36.

Chapter 5
Knowledge Requirements of DERESIS Model

Ergonomics uses different disciplinary knowledge as an aim to plan, design, manage, and continuously improve the work systems to be productive, efficient, and to be human-oriented (Schlick et al. 2010). In the following chapter, the required knowledge, which is multidisciplinary, is introduced to develop the model. The required methods cover three aspects: technical, organizational, and human science perspectives (see Table 5.1).

5.1 Fuzzy Linguistics Theory

Zadeh (1975a) introduced the fuzzy set theory to enable uncertain and imprecise real world systems to be captured by linguistic variables. Fuzzy logic is therefore a useful tool for dealing with decisions involving complex, ambiguous, and vague phenomena based on the meanings of the linguistic variables. Traditional quantitative methods are problematic when analysing complicated and ill-defined situations. The study by Zadeh (1975b) describes the solution as the fuzzy linguistic method. The fuzzy linguistic approach is an approximate technique which represents qualitative aspects as linguistic values by means of linguistic variables (Zadeh 1975c). Linguistic expression provides a useful approach for interpreting the semantics of vagueness based on the subjective judgments of evaluators. Linguistic variables are variables which do not bear numerical values, but are words or sentences in a natural or artificial language. The concept of linguistic variables has been developed as a counterpart to the concept of a numerical variables (Lin et al. 2013).

Fuzzy theory constructs a conceptual framework for a systematic treatment of fuzziness in linguistic variables that are represented in words or sentences. These linguistic variables are interpreted as fuzzy sets, characterised by membership functions. A fuzzy set is a mapping of a set of real numbers onto membership values that lie in the range [0,1]. Membership function can capture the human

Q. Lin, *Analysis of Resource Management in Complex Work Systems*,
DOI 10.1007/978-981-10-2170-1_5

Table 5.1 The required methods derived from three aspects

Three aspects	Method
Technical perspectives	Fuzzy linguistics theory
	Balanced Scorecard
Organizational perspectives	Networked thinking
	Change management
Human science perspectives	Group research • Group decision making • Communication in group • Collaboration

quantitative meaning of such variables so they can be processed as data. To capture the true human meaning of words or sentences, constructing their membership functions is important for the success of fuzzy applications (Lin et al. 2013).

The objective of a fuzzy linguistic approach is to solve complicated, subjective and undefined situations. The fuzzy linguistic variables are adapted to triangular fuzzy numbers which are classified to symmetry. Linguistic variables are triangular fuzzy numbers, no matter whether they are symmetric, and have similar estimated results. There is no difference between using symmetric or asymmetric triangular fuzzy numbers in research (Wu et al. 2010).

The linguistic scale given in Fig. 5.1 is used for the evaluation, since people usually use linguistic terms to define their logical judgements (Olcer and Odabasi 2005). Figure 5.1 shows triangular fuzzy numbers for the intangible linguistic scale where linguistic terms are defined as very poor (VP), poor (P), fair (F), good (G), very good (VG). The corresponding fuzzy numbers of the five linguistic scale are (0,0,15), (10,25,40), (35,50,65), (60,75,90), (85,100,100).

To weight the importance for each criterion, it is described with a five-scale fuzzy linguistic: absolutely unimportant (AU), unimportant (U), moderately

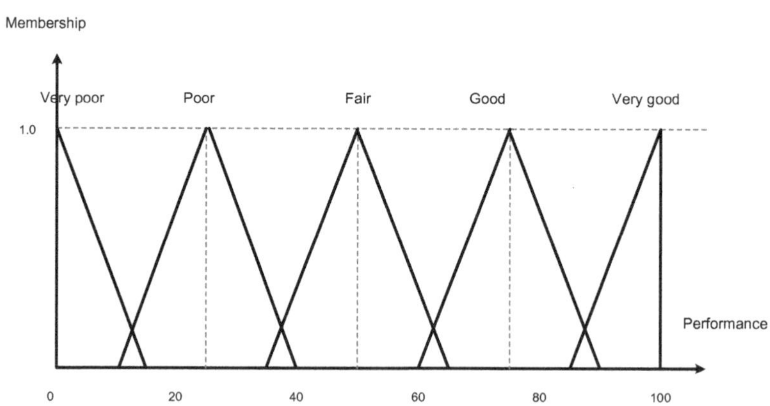

Fig. 5.1 Fuzzy linguistic values of performance. *Source* Lin et al. (2013)

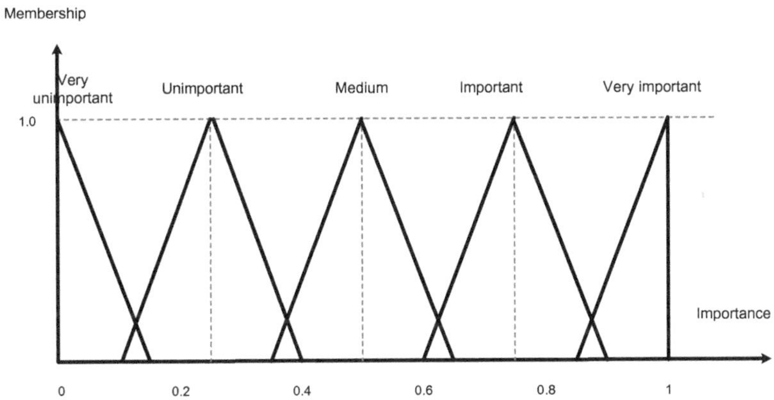

Fig. 5.2 Fuzzy linguistic values of importance. *Source* Lin et al. (2013)

important (MI), important (I), and very important (VI) (Fig. 5.2), where the corresponding fuzzy numbers are (0,0,0.15), (0.1,0.25,0.4), (0.35,0.5,0.65), (0.6,0.75,0.9), (0.85,1,1), respectively.

Let P_{ij}^{m} be the performance value evaluated by expert m for perspective i and criterion j, and the membership function of triangular fuzzy number $P_{ij}^{m} \in T$. Let I_{ij}^{m} be the weight of importance evaluated by respondent m for perspective i and criterion j, and the membership function of triangular fuzzy number $I_{ij}^{m} \in S$.

$$P_{ij}^{m} = \left(LP_{ij}^{m}, MP_{ij}^{m}, UP_{ij}^{m}\right), V_{ij}^{m} \in T, \quad \text{where } 0 \le LP_{ij}^{m} \le MP_{ij}^{m} \le UP_{ij}^{m} \le 100 \tag{5.1}$$

$$I_{ij}^{m} = \left(LI_{ij}^{m}, MI_{ij}^{m}, UI_{ij}^{m}\right), I_{ij}^{m} \in S, \quad \text{where } 0 \le LI_{ij}^{m} \le MI_{ij}^{m} \le UI_{ij}^{m} \le 1 \tag{5.2}$$

Equations (5.3) and (5.4) are used to aggregate the expert opinions of performance value and importance.

$$P_{ij} = P_{ij}^{1} * W_{e1} + P_{ij}^{2} * W_{e2} + \cdots + P_{ij}^{m} * W_{em} \tag{5.3}$$

$$I_{ij} = I_{ij}^{1} * W_{e1} + I_{ij}^{2} * W_{e2} + \cdots + I_{ij}^{m} * W_{m2} \tag{5.4}$$

where P_{ij}, I_{ij}, W_{em} and m are the value of expert opinion for perspective i and criterion j, the importance of expert opinion for perspective i and criterion j, expert weight and number of expert in performance evaluation group, respectively.

Since the output of the fuzzy system is a fuzzy set, the defuzzification procedure is used to convert the fuzzy result into a numerical value. Mean-of-maximum (MOM) defuzzification and centre-of-area (COA) defuzzification are popular methods which convert a fuzzy set to a non-fuzzy value. Braae and Rutherford (1978), Runkler and

Glesner (1993) compared these two defuzzification methods and concluded that COA yields better results than MOM (Wu et al. 2010). The COA is a simple and practical method for calculating the NBSC value. Equations (5.5) and (5.6) show the NBSC values of fuzzy performance and fuzzy weight, respectively.

$$\mathrm{NBSC}_i^p = \frac{[(\mathrm{UP_i} - \mathrm{LP_i}) + (\mathrm{MP_i} - \mathrm{LP_i})]}{3} + \mathrm{LP_i}\ \forall \mathrm{i} \tag{5.5}$$

$$\mathrm{NBSC}_i^I = \frac{[(\mathrm{UI_i} - \mathrm{LI_i}) + (\mathrm{MI_i} - \mathrm{LI_i})]}{3} + \mathrm{LI_i}\ \forall \mathrm{i} \tag{5.6}$$

5.2 Balanced Scorecard

For decades, managers of an organization focused primarily on measuring and controlling financial performance, but now they are increasingly recognizing the need to assess other aspects of performance. They know that their organization must develop the capabilities which it will need to prosper in the future (Daft 2001). The Balanced Scorecard (BSC) integrates the various dimensions of control, so that managers have a complete picture of organizational performance. It has become the core management system for many organizations, e.g. business and industry, government, and non-profit organizations. They align business activities to the vision and strategy of the organization, improve internal and external communications, and monitor organizational performance against strategic goals (Lin et al. 2013). BSC helps managers understand many interrelationships. This understanding can help managers transcend traditional notions about functional barriers, and leads ultimately to improved decision making and problem solving (Kaplan and Norton 1992). The components of BSC are designed in an integrated manner so that they reinforce one another, and link short-term actions with long-term strategic goals (Daft 2001). Managers can use BSC to set goals, allocate resources, plan budgets, and determine rewards (Stewart and Carpenter-Hubin 2000; Kettunen and Kantola 2005).

BSC was originally developed by Kaplan and Norton as a performance measurement tool for managers to obtain a quick, yet comprehensive view of how their businesses were operating (Kaplan and Norton 1992). It is a management concept that links strategic management with operational business processes through a balanced panel of financial and non-financial data. Thus the day-to-day direction of the company, with all its successful factors for every manager and employee is understood in a tangible way (Lange 2004). The success of BSC or a similar device will depend on the clear identification of non-financial and financial variables, their accurate and objective measurement, and linking performance to rewards and penalties. The aim of BSC is to direct and help manage change in support of the long term strategy, in order to manage performance. In general, a BSC system is considered to be a performance measurement system, a strategy evaluation system, and a communication tool. It translates mission and strategy into objectives and measures, and is divided into four different perspectives: the financial perspective, the customer perspective, the internal processes perspective, and the learning and growth perspective (Kaplan and Norton 1996a; Ehrmann 2000). Kaplan and Norton (1996b) argued that the BSC program is a cause-and-effect relationship between different measurements in the selected perspective, as Fig. 5.3 shows.

The financial perspective is regularly represented by data describing the economic results of previous activities. The financial objectives serve as a focus for the objectives and performance indicators for all other scorecard perspectives (Conrad 2001). Each selected measure should be part of the cause and effect chain which leads eventually to the improvement of the financial result. Financial goals at every stage of the life cycle of a company can be quite different. In the growth phase, the central financial goal should be revenue growth in target markets. In the mature phase, the company expects an excellent return on investment (ROI). In the decline phase, the focus is on cash flow (Wagner 2002). However, the situation can change quickly within a phase. In a decline phase, sudden growth can arise by e.g. a change in technology or statutory provisions. Therefore, the strategic framework of each phase should be reviewed periodically, and a change of strategy made where necessary. According to Kaplan and Norton, financial goals and metrics play a dual role (Müller 2000):

- On the one hand, they define the financial performance that is expected of the selected strategy.
- On the other hand, they serve as the ultimate goals for the goals and metrics of the other scorecard perspectives.

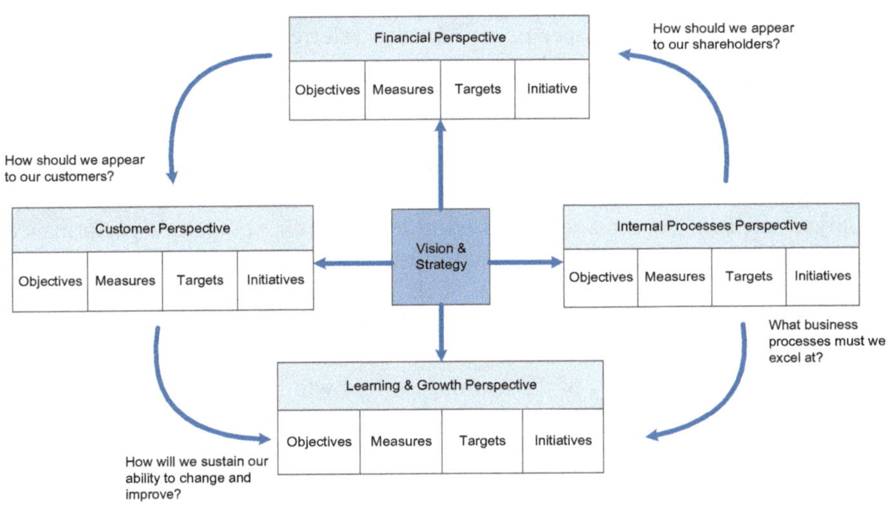

Fig. 5.3 The cause and effect of BSC. *Source* Adopted from Kaplan and Norton (1992)

The Financial perspective should show the results of the strategic choices made in the other perspectives, while at the same time establishing several long-term goals, thus a large part of the general ground rules and premises for the other perspectives (Olve et al. 1999).

In the customer perspective, the customer and market segments are identified and defined. This perspective describes the ways in which value is to be created for customers, how customer demand for this value is to be satisfied, and why the customer will be willing to pay for it (Olve et al. 1999). The customer perspective emphasizes customer satisfaction. Recent management philosophy has shown an increasing realization of the importance of customer satisfaction in any business. If customers are not satisfied, they will eventually find other suppliers who will meet their needs. The indicators in the customer perspective are often:

- Market share,
- Customer satisfaction,
- Customer loyalty,
- Customer retention and new customer acquisition,
- Profitability per customer.

The internal processes perspective refers to internal business processes. For the BSC, a complete value chain of internal processes should be defined. The complete value chain of internal processes must be linked to both the customer perspective and the financial perspective (Conrad 2001). The value chain of internal processes begins with the identification of emerging or latent customer needs, which the company must explore in the innovation process. It continues in the operation process with which products and services are created and delivered to the customer. Metrics based on this perspective allow the managers to know how well their business is running, and whether its products and services conform to customer requirements.

The learning and growth perspective is also referred to as an innovation perspective. In the information age, investment in people, systems and processes seems to be more important than investment in fixed assets. Companies have recognized that employees, who work directly with internal processes and customers, represent their most important asset. The employee-related indicators can be: employee satisfaction, staff loyalty and employee productivity (Conrad 2001). In particular, employee satisfaction seems to be a driving force for the company's performance. And employee training is also important in the information society. In the current climate of rapid technological change, it is becoming necessary for knowledge workers to be in a continuous learning mode. In any case, learning and growth constitute the essential foundation for the success of any knowledge-worker organization. The objectives of the learning and growth perspective are the driving factors for excellent results for the first three scorecard perspectives (Kaplan and Norton 1997).

Within these four areas, managers identify key performance indicators which the organization will track, generally limiting the number of measures to five per area for a total of twenty control metrics. BSC gives us a valuable tool for enabling employees to understand the company's situation. This is essential if the company is to achieve the dynamism it needs to be competitive in the long run. It also provides us with useful documentation for continually developing those control measures which will most quickly guide the company towards achieving its goals and its vision. Table 5.2 provides an overview of this process and also indicates the nature of the work and the time required for each step. As previously noted, the exact arrangement, and thus the time allotted, must be adapted to the characteristics and situation for each company (Olve et al. 1999).

Table 5.2 The step in the building process of balanced scorecard

Step	Description	Procedure	Suggested time
1	Define the industry, describe its development and the role of the company	Interviews with as many people as possible. Should be done if possible by an outside party to obtain the most objective picture. Research on industry situation and trends	1–2 months
2	Establish/confirm the company's vision	Joint seminar attended by top management and opinion leaders	1–2 meetings of 1.5 days each
3	Establish the perspectives	Seminar attended by top management, the project group, and someone having previous experience with balanced scorecard projects	1–2 days
4	Break the vision down according to each perspective and formulate overall strategic goals	Joint seminar with the same group as in step 2	See below
5	Identify critical factors for success	At the seminar above	Total including step 4: 2–3 days
6	Develop measures, identify causes and effects and establish a balance	At the seminar above, if possible. However, a certain interval is often beneficial	Included above, otherwise 1–2 days
7	Establish the top level scorecard	Final determination by top management and the project group. Preferably, though, with the participation of someone having previous experience with balanced scorecard projects	1–2 days

(continued)

Table 5.2 (continued)

Step	Description	Procedure	Suggested time
8	Breakdown of the scorecard and measures by organizational unit	Suitable for a project divided up into appropriate organizational units under the leadership of the project group. Preferably all personnel involved should take part in the project work of each unit; a suitable form for the work would be a seminar. Progress reports and ongoing coordination with top management. Help from an experienced balanced scorecard architect is especially important in aligning success factors and measures	Total of 2 months and upward. For each local seminar, at least ½–1 day
9	Formulate goals	Proposals by each unit project leader. Final approval of goals by top management	No estimate
10	Develop an action plan	Prepared by each project group	No estimate
11	Implementing the scorecard	Ensured by ongoing monitoring under the overall responsibility of top management	No estimate

5.3 Networked Thinking

There are three different types of problem situation to be considered: simple, complicated and complex. Simple problems have few influence variables, relationships and interactions. Although complicated problem situations have many factors and links, they have few movements or dynamics. Complex problem situations are characterized by high dynamics, which exist along with many different factors. Complex problem situations have increased enormously and gained importance in recent years (Probst and Gomez 1991).

The environment, in which organizations operate, and their activities have become increasingly complex. It is highly networked and has become more dynamic. The hierarchical organization principle has lost much of its meaning. As science and technology develops in the information age, our society depends more on a diversity of networks (Li et al. 2007). Network theory is a way for mapping and managing substantive, strategic and institutional uncertainties in a complex system. The network approach provides theoretical concepts and starting points for analyzing and evaluating the complex processes of problem solving and decision making. Moreover, it provides a prescription for improving the interactions between parties and management strategies for initiating and supporting these interactions (Koppenjan and Klijn 2004).

Networked thinking is used to describe, (i) the research into complexity, (ii) the inherent rule of dynamics by means of the basic theory of complex networks, and (iii) the representation of novel knowledge with network topology (Li et al. 2007). It has been researched in two main respects: nodes, and the interaction between nodes (Li et al. 2007).

The problem solving methodology of networked thinking helps not only to obtain more comprehensive solutions, but also to allow personnel to deal with complex situations reliably. Intuition is not enough, but procedural steps are available which will recognize the connections, dynamic, behavioral patterns, limits and possibilities of steering, and the developing and learning skills (Probst and Gomez 1991).

Essentially, situations are defined from different perspectives. This achieves a more adequate definition of the problem. The relationships and their features are presented and analyzed in networked form, with the way in which behavioral patterns are developed and interpreted. This step of the methodology for networked thinking is outlined in Fig. 5.4 (Probst and Gomez 1991).

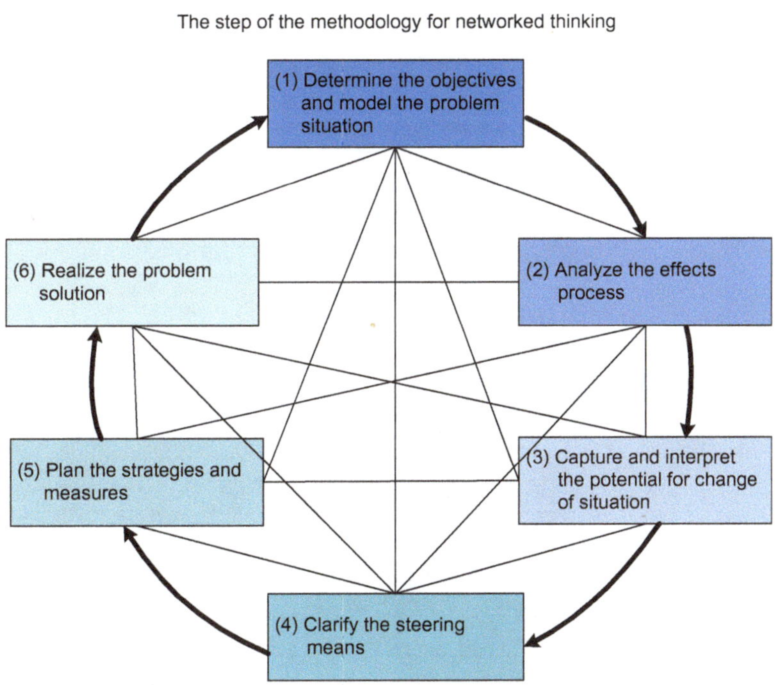

Fig. 5.4 The steps of the methodology of networked thinking. *Source* Probst and Gomez (1991)

The steps listed here are treated in a linear manner and described briefly. However, it is more practical to deal with it in an iterative and networked process. This means that, for example, returning to the problem description, it may be necessary to obtain more information or reconsider strategies, if the network undergoes a substantial change, or early warning indicators need to be incorporated into the network etc. (Probst and Gomez 1991).

5.4 Change Management

Social entities such as enterprises, industries, national and regional economies are often characterized by "dynamics", "turbulence", "transformation" or "discontinuity". Change serves as an umbrella term for all these significant and sometimes dramatic transitions. Changes affecting people management take place on at least three levels (see Fig. 5.5) (Reiß 2012).

On the organization level, change affects all sectors of an enterprise. The spectrum of organizational change (see Fig. 5.6) ranges from a change in strategies,

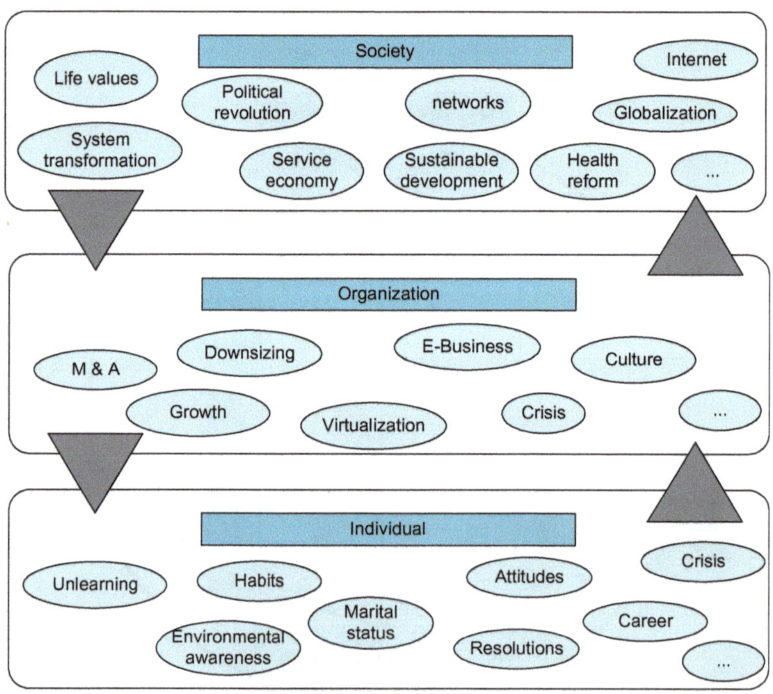

Fig. 5.5 Levels of change. *Source* Reiß (2012)

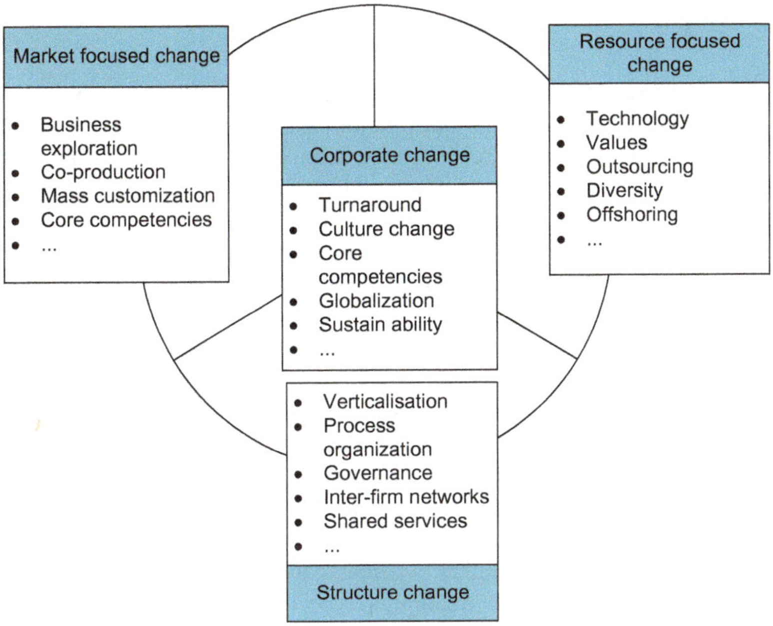

Fig. 5.6 Sectors of organizational change. *Source* Reiß (2012)

to human resources, technologies and systems, structures, and to cultures (Reiß 2012).

Change is an ever-present element that affects all organizations (Todnem By 2005). The successful management of change is crucial to any organization in order to survive and succeed in the highly competitive and continuously evolving business environment (Todnem By 2005).

Change management is a systematic approach to developing individuals, teams, and organizations from their current state to a desired future state (Wikipedia 2013), it is the process of continually renewing an organization's direction, structure, and capabilities, in order to serve the ever-changing needs of external and internal customers (Moran and Brightman 2001). Change management has three different aspects: adapting to change, controlling change, and effecting change. For an organization, change management means defining and implementing procedures and/or technologies to deal with changes in the business environment and to profit from changing opportunities (Rouse 2010). The goal of change management is to maximize benefits and to minimize the impact change has on workers (Kotter 2011).

Change management can be divided into four main topics:

- Development and implementation of vision
- Communication with all the persons concerned
- Participation of the persons concerned
- The qualification of the persons concerned.

5.5 Group Research

A group is composed of two or more individuals who are connected by and within social relationships. It has more information and a greater capacity to process information (Forsyth 2010). Work organizations consist of individuals, but typically these individuals are formed into particular work groups. Groups are very important to the functioning of work organizations. They not only help to provide professional identities for their members and satisfy human needs for social interaction and the development of interpersonal work relationships, but they also help to establish rules for proper behavior in the work setting, and they play a part in determining the courses of action that the work group and the organization will follow (Riggio 2013).

There are many goal-related activities which groups undertake. McGrath's (1984) circumplex model of group tasks distinguishes four basic group goals (see Fig. 5.7): generating ideas or plans, choosing a solution, negotiating a solution to a conflict, or executing a task. Each of these basic goals can be further subdivided, yielding a total of eight basic goal-related activities. Tasks in the upper four quadrants (type 1,2,3,8) require cooperation among members, whereas conflict is more likely when groups undertake those tasks in the lower quadrants (type 4,5,6,7). Tasks on the right side of

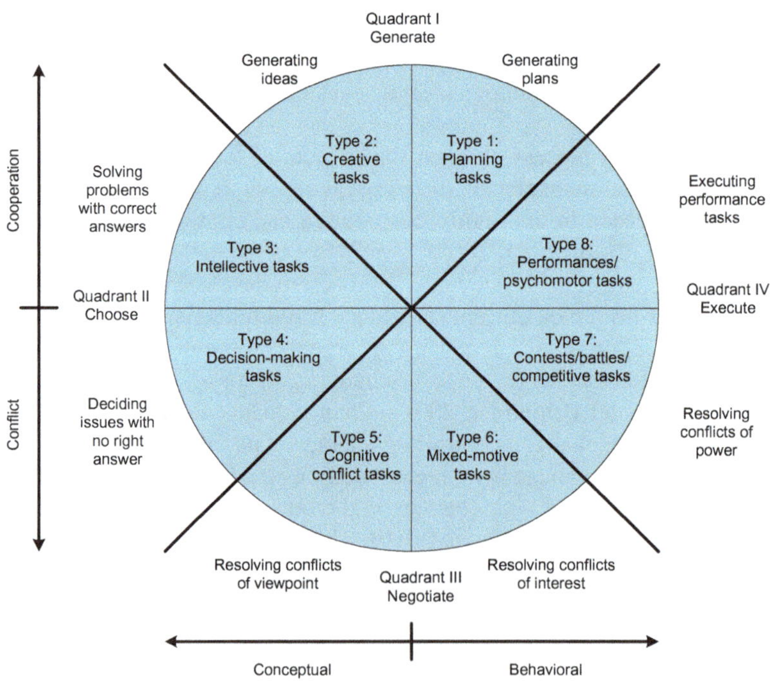

Fig. 5.7 McGrath's task circumplex model of group tasks. *Source* McGrath (1984)

the circle (type 1,6,7,8) are behavioral ones, whereas those on the left side (type 2,3,4,5) are more intellectual, conceptual tasks (Forsyth 2010).

5.5.1 Group Decision Making

In recent years, organizations have been turning more and more to group strategies for making important work-related decisions. The group decision making process is one of the most important processes in work groups. It includes establishing group goals, choosing from various courses of action, selecting new members, and determining standards of appropriate behavior. There are three strategies for group decision making i.e. autocratic decision making, democratic decision making, and consensus decision making (Riggio 2013).

In most cases, groups are better at choosing, judging, estimating, and problem solving than are individuals (Stasser and Dietz-Uhler 2001). Although group decision making has many advantages, it also has some disadvantages (see Table 5.3) (Riggio 2013).

Skill decision making groups are more likely to make use of group procedures that enhance the way they gather, analyze, and weight up information. There are four main stages in the group decision making process, i.e. orientation, discussion, decision, and implementation. The functional theory of group decision making is shown in Fig. 5.8 (Forsyth 2010).

Group decision making has been commended as a panacea for overcoming increasingly complex tasks, for solving social conflicts, and for securing cooperation (Brandstätter 1982).

5.5.2 Communication Within the Group

Communication is the activity of transferring information through the exchange of thoughts, messages, or information, using speech, visuals, signals, writing, or behavior from one person or group to another person or group. Communication involves the exchange of information between two or more parties. This is best represented by a simple model of communication between two persons: the sender and the receiver (Riggio 2013). The process of communication is described in

Table 5.3 The advantages and disadvantages of group decision making

Advantages	Disadvantages
Works from a broad knowledge base	Slow (can be a problem in crisis situation)
Decision is accepted by members	Creates intergroup conflict
Decision is highly critiqued	Potential for groupthink and group polarization
Aspects of the problem can be divided among group members	Certain members, such as leaders, may dominate the decision making process

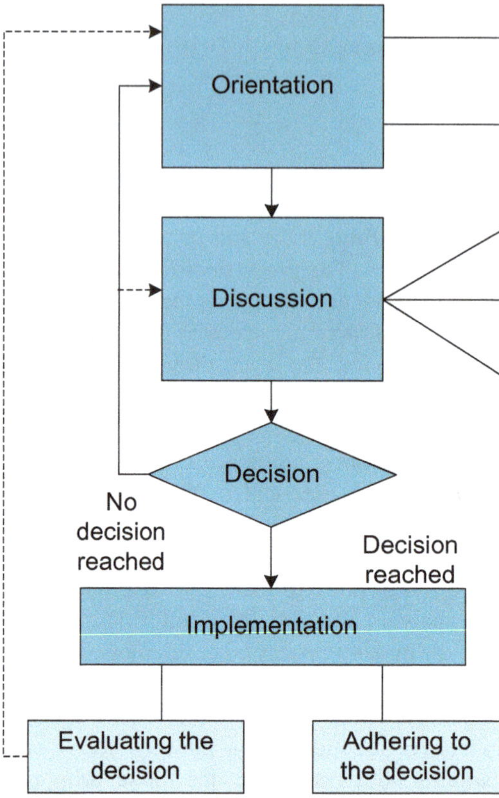

Fig. 5.8 A functional model of group decision making. *Source* Forsyth (2010)

Fig. 5.9. Errors in communication could occur at any stage. Communication begins with some information—a message—that the sender wishes to transmit to a receiver. The task of the sender is to take the information and select a channel to transmit the message from the sender to the receiver.

Communication channels or methods of communication are the means by which messages are transmitted (Berger and Iyengar 2013). The channels are the vehicles, through which messages will be transmitted from the sender to the receiver. The sender may choose the spoken word, either face-to-face or by telephone, or the written word, using a memo or a typed message sent through a computerized mail network. Different methods of communication have various advantages and disadvantages (see Table 5.4) (Riggio 2013). With spoken communication, the noise could produce a signal distortion at any stage. There are three aspects of noise which are of importance to Human Factors Engineering (HFE), i.e. the stray or unwanted signal component, the high-volume of background noise, and the psychological stress (Guastello 2006).

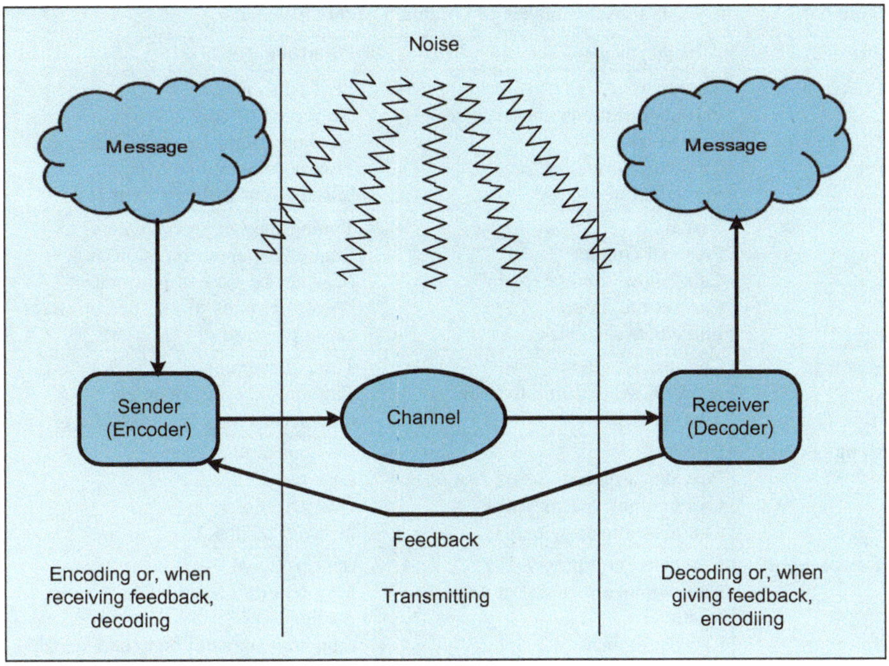

Fig. 5.9 The communication process. *Source* Riggio (2013)

Communication is the medium for the coordination and control of, for example, group activities, member socialization, group integration, and conflict management (Poole and Hirokawa 1996). Group communication is a means for providing multipoint to multipoint communication, by organizing processes in groups (Chockler et al. 2001). Group communication has been proven to be difficult to understand. The interaction of multiple parties subject to manifold psychological, social, and contextual influences is one of the most difficult topics of study in the human sciences (Poole and Hirokawa 1996). Communication within a group is a necessary precondition for high-quality group decision making. It has the greatest impact on decision making performance in a complex, interdependent, and equivocal environment (Hirokawa 1990).

5.5.3 Collaboration

Collaboration deals with the relations and interactions between co-workers. Collaboration is a complex, voluntary and dynamic process involving several skills. Some keywords outline the complexity of the concept of collaboration: sharing, partnership, interdependency and power (D'Amour et al. 2005). Sharing is a concept used by most researchers. Partnership implies two or more individuals joining

Table 5.4 Advantages and disadvantages of communication channels

Channel	Advantages	Disadvantages
Telephone	Verbal Permits questions and answers Convenient Two-way flow Immediate feedback	Less personal No record of conversation Message might be misunderstood Timing may be inconvenient May be impossible to terminate
Face-to-face	Visual Personal contact Can "show" and "explain" Can set the mood Immediate feedback	Timing may be inconvenient Requires spontaneous thinking May not be easy to terminate Power or status of one person may cause pressure
Meetings	Can use visuals Involves several minds at once Two-way flow	Time consuming Time may be inconvenient One person may dominate the group
Memorandum	Brief Provides a record Can prethink the message Can disseminate widely	No control over receiver Less personal One-way flow Delayed feedback
Formal report	Complete; comprehensive Can organize material at writer's leisure Can disseminate widely	Less personal May require considerable time in reading Language may not be understandable Expensive One-way flow Delayed feedback
Teleconference	Saves traveling time Visual Reduce costs Help users to be better prepared	Miss interpersonal contact Not good for initial brainstorming sessions Expensive
Electronic mail	Convenient Messages sent/received at all hours Extremely fast compared to other written messages Can be sent to multiple parties simultaneously	Ease can lead to message "overload" No nonverbal communication Other may be able to get access to messages
Web-based	Convenient Can interact in real time Can communicate with multiple parties simultaneously Can present drawings/figures easily	Ease can lead to message "overload" Difficult to control flow of messages (e.g., turn-taking)

in a collaborative undertaking where the partners pursue a common goal, a set of shared goals or specific outcomes. Interdependency infers that there is a mutual dependency, which maximizes the contribution of an individual. The fourth concept is power, which is considered to be shared between team members (D'Amour et al. 2004). Collaboration is an important factor for achieving goals in productivity, quality and knowledge sharing (Magdaleno et al. 2012).

Fig. 5.10 The collaboration model. *Source* Kim (2010)

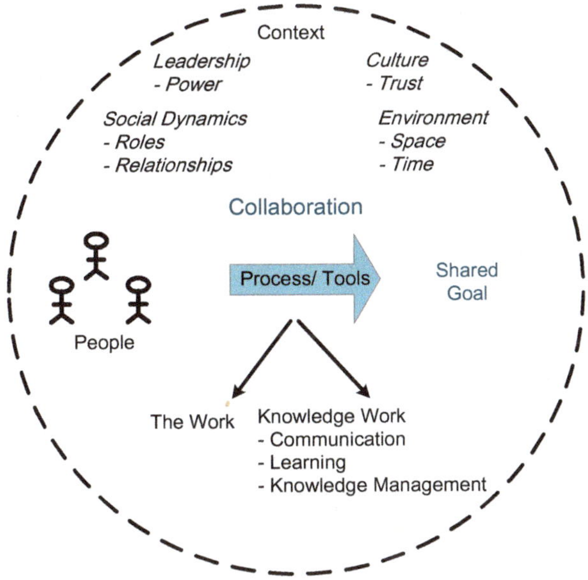

Various researchers see collaboration as a dynamic or interactive process, a transforming process, or an interpersonal process (Nolte 2005; Thomson and Perry 2006). Gray (1989) describes collaboration as "*a process through which parties who see different aspects of a problem can constructively explore their differences and search for solutions that go beyond their own limited vision of what is possible*". Chrislip and Larson (1994) introduce the process as "*a mutually beneficial relationship between two or more parties who work toward common goals by sharing responsibility, authority, and accountability for achieving results. The purpose of collaboration is to create a shared vision and joint strategies to address concerns that go beyond the purview of any particular party.*"

Kim (2010) proposes the model of collaboration (see Fig. 5.10). The context of collaboration includes: leadership, culture, social dynamics, and environment. Collaboration is defined as: two or more people working together through the process or using some tools to seek a shared, collective, and bounded goal.

Collaboration taking place in the human context is described as "team working". There are various terms to qualify teams, the most common being interdisciplinary collaboration (D'Amour et al. 2004). Interdisciplinary collaboration has been put forward as a way to improve decision making in health care systems and has been recommended for improving health care itself. With collaboration there is the sharing of information and perspectives. More studies of interdisciplinary bioethical decision making are needed (Baggs 1993).

Interdisciplinary collaboration in health care systems results in improved coordination of care between different groups of professionals. This collaboration aims at working in parallel with normal practice. Professionals would continue to pursue their goals, with little co-ordination or sharing of responsibilities and tasks with other work group members (Sicotte et al. 2002). Interdisciplinary collaboration is a main factor in the initiatives designed to increase the effectiveness of health services (D'Amour et al. 2005).

References

Baggs, J. G. (1993). Collaborative interdisciplinary bioethical decision making in intensive care units. *Nursing Outlook, 41*(3), 108–112.

Berger, J., & Iyengar, R. (2013). Communication channels and word of mouth: how the medium shapes the message. *Journal of Consumer Research, 40*. Retrieved September 30, 2013, from https://www.google.de/url?sa=t&rctj&q=&esrc=s&frm=1&source=web&cd=2&cad=rja&ved=0CDkQFjAB&url=https%3A%2F%2Fmarketing.wharton.upenn.edu%2Ffiles%2F%3Fwhdmsaction%3Dpublic%3Amain.file%26fileID%3D6146&ei=TuJKUuiWK8jJsgaiyoGwBA&usg=AFQjCNGKnVJpWRZiWabVNMlFczVCr8PI8g&sig2=fQrhQCdx36dfyMk6cXysFg&bvm=bv.53371865,d.Yms

Braae, M., & Rutherford, D. A. (1978). Fuzzy relations in a control setting. *Kybernetes, 7*(3), 185–188.

Brandstätter, H. (1982). Recent research on group decision making. In H. Brandstätter, J. H. Davis, & G. Stocker-Kreichgauer (Eds.), *Group decision making*. New York: Academic Press.

Chockler, G. V., Keidar, I., & Vitenberg, R. (2001). Group communication specifications: A comprehensive study. *ACM Computing Surveys, 33*(4), 427–469.

Chrislip, D. D., & Larson, C. E. (1994). *Collaborative leadership: How citizens and civic leaders can make a difference*. San Francisco: Jossey-Bass Inc.

Conrad, H. J. (2001). *Balanced scorecard als modernes management-instrument im Krankenhaus*. Kulmbach: Baumann Fachverlag.

Daft, R. L. (2001). *Organization theory and design* (7th ed.). Cincinnati: South-Western College Publishing.

D'Amour, D., Beaulieu, M. D., Rodriguez, L. S. M., & Ferrada-Videla, M. (2004). Key elements of collaborative practice & frameworks: conceptual basis for interdisciplinary practice. In: *Interdisciplinary Education for Collaborative, Patient-Centred Practice*. Research and Findings Report, Canada. Retrieved January 23, 2013, from http://www.ferasi.umontreal.ca/eng/07_info/IECPCP_Final_Report.pdf

D'Amour, D., Ferrada-Videla, M., Rodriguez, L. S. M., & Beaulieu, M. D. (2005). The conceptual basis for interprofessional collaboration: Core concepts and theoretical frameworks. *Journal of Interprofessional Care, Supplement, 1*, 116–131.

Ehrmann, H. (2000). *Kompakt- Training Balanced Scorecard*. Ludwigshafen: Friedrich Kiehl Verlag.

Forsyth, D. R. (2010). *Group dynamics* (5th ed.). Belmont: Wadsworth, Cengage Learning.

Gray, B. (1989). *Collaborating: Finding common ground for multiparty problems*. San Francisco: Jossey-Bass.

Guastello, S. J. (2006). *Human factors engineering and ergonomics: A systems approach*. New Jersey: Lawrence Erlbaum Associates.

Hirokawa, R. Y. (1990). The role of communication in group decision making efficacy: A task-contingency perspective. *Small Group Research, 21*(2), 190–204.

Kaplan, R. S., & Norton, D. P. (1992). The balanced scorecard-measures that drive performance. *Harvard Business Review, 70*(1), 71–79.

Kaplan, R. S., & Norton, D. P. (1996a). Using the balanced scorecard as a strategic management system. *Harvard Business Review, 74*(1), 75–85.

Kaplan, R. S., & Norton, D. P. (1996b). *The balanced scorecard: Translating strategy into action*. Boston: Harvard Business School Press.

Kaplan, R. S., & Norton, D. P. (1997). Balanced scorecard: Strategien erfolgreich umsetzen, aus dem amerikanischen übersetzt von Horvath, P., Kuhn-Würfel, B. & Vogelhuber, C. Stuttgart: Schäffer- Poeschel Verlag.

Kettunen, J., & Kantola, I. (2005). Management information system based on the balanced scorecard. *Campus Wide Information Systems, 22*(5), 263–274.

Kim, E. (2010). *What is collaboration?* Retrieved April 13, 2013, from http://www.slideshare.net/eekim/collaboration-model

Koppenjan, J., & Klijn, E. H. (2004). *Managing uncertainties in networks: A network approach to problem solving and decision making*. New York: Taylor & Francis Group.

Kotter, J. (2011). *Change management vs. change leadership—What's the difference?* Retrieved December 13, 2012, from http://www.forbes.com/sites/johnkotter/2011/07/12/change-management-vs-change-leadership-whats-the-difference/

Lange, O. (2004). *Balanced scorecard – Ein Managementkonzept für deutsche Buchverlage*. London: Holger Ehling Publishing.

Li, D. Y., Xiao, L. P., Han, Y. N., Chen, G. S., & Liu, K. (2007). Network thinking and network intelligence. In N. Zhong, J. M. Liu, Y. Y. Yao, J. L. Wu, S. F. Lu, & K. C. Li (Eds.), *Web intelligence meets brain informatics, First WICI International Workshop, WImBI 2006*. Berlin, Heidelberg: Springer.

Lin, Q. L., Liu, L., Liu, H. C., & Wang, D. J. (2013). Integrating hierarchical balanced scorecard with fuzzy linguistic for evaluating operating room performance in hospitals. *Expert Systems with Applications, 40*(6), 1917–1924.

Magdaleno, A. M., Araujo, R. M., & Werner, C. M. L. (2012). An exploratory study on collaboration understanding in software development social networks. In V. Herskovic, H. U. Hoppe, M. Jansen, & J. Ziegler (Eds.), *Collaboration and Technology—18th International Conference, CRIWG 2012*. Heidelberg: Springer.

McGrath, J. E. (1984). *Groups: Interaction and performance*. New Jersey: Prentice Hall.

Moran, J. M., & Brightman, B. K. (2001). Leading organizational change. *Career Development International, 6*(2), 111–118.

Müller, A. (2000). *Strategisches Management mit der Balanced Scorecard*. Stuttgart: W. Kohlhammer.

Nolte, J. (2005). *Enhancing interdisciplinary collaboration in primary health care in Canada*. Retrieved March 24, 2013, from http://www.eicp.ca/en/resources/pdfs/enhancing-interdisciplinary-collaboration-in-primary-health-care-in-canada.phd

Olcer, A. I., & Odabasi, A. Y. (2005). A new fuzzy multiple attributive group decision making methodology and its application to propulsion/maneuvering system selection problem. *European Journal of Operational Research, 166*(1), 93–114.

Olve, N. G., Roy, J., & Wetter, M. (1999). *Performance drivers: A practical guide to using the balanced scorecard*. Chichester: Wiley.

Poole, M. S., & Hirokawa, R. Y. (1996). Introduction communication and group decision making. In: R. Y. Hirokawa & M. S. Poole (Eds.), *Communication and group decision making*, 2nd ed. California: Sage Publications.

Probst, G. J. B., & Gomez, P. (1991). Die Methodik des Vernetzten Denkens zur Loesung komplexer Probleme. In: Probst, G.J.B. & Gomez, P. (Hrsg.), *Vernetztes Denken – Ganzheitliches Fuehren in der Praxis. 2. Erweiterte Auflage*. Wiesbaden: Gabler Verlag.

Reiß, M. (2012). *Change management: A balanced and blended approach*. Norderstedt: Demand GmbH.

Riggio, R. E. (2013). *Introduction to industrial/organizational psychology* (6th ed.). New Jersey: Pearson Education.

Rouse, M. (2010). *Definition change management*. Retrieved January 15, 2013, from http://searchcio-midmarket.techtarget.com/definition/change-management

Runkler, T. A., & Glesner, M. (1993). A set of axioms for defuzzification strategies towards a theory of rational defuzzification operators. In: *Second IEEE International Conference on Fuzzy Systems*, San Diego.

Schlick, C. M., Bruder, R., & Luczak, H. (2010). *Arbeitswissenschaft, 3., vollst. überarb. und erw. Aufl.* Berlin, Heidelberg: Springer.

Sicotte, C., D'Amour, D., & Moreault, M. P. (2002). Interdisciplinary collaboration within Quebec community health care centres. *Social Science and Medicine, 55*, 991–1003.

Stasser, G., & Dietz-Uhler, B. (2001). Collective choice, judgment, and problem solving. In M. A. Hogg & R. S. Tindale (Eds.), *Blackwell handbook of social psychology: Group processes*. Malden: Blackwell.

Stewart, A. C., & Carpenter-Hubin, J. (2000). The balanced scorecard: Beyond reports and rankings. *Planning for Higher Education*. Retrieved June 12, 2013, from https://mail.csuchico.edu/vpaa/vpprae/docs/pdf/BSC-stewartcarpenter-hubin.pdf

Thomson, A. M., & Perry, J. L. (2006). *Collaboration processes: Inside the black box* (pp. 20–32). Special Issue: Public Administration Review.

Todnem By, R. (2005). Organizational change management: A critical review. *Journal of Change Management, 5*(4), 369–380.

Wagner, J. (2002). *Balanced Scorecard als Managementsystem*. Köln: Josef Eul Verlag.

Wikipedia. (2013). *Change management*. Retrieved April 10, 2013, from http://en.wikipedia.org/wiki/Change_management

Wu, C. T., Tsai, H. T., Shih, M. H., & Fu, H. H. (2010). Government performance evaluation using a balanced scorecard with a fuzzy linguistic scale. *The Service Industries Journal, 30*(3), 449–462.

Zadeh, L. A. (1975a). The concept of a linguistic variables and its application to approximate reasoning. *Parts I. Information Sciences, 8*(2), 199–249.

Zadeh, L. A. (1975b). The concept of a linguistic variables and its application to approximate reasoning. *Parts II. Information Sciences, 8*(3), 301–357.

Zadeh, L. A. (1975c). The concept of a linguistic variables and its application to approximate reasoning. *Parts III. Information Sciences, 9*(1), 43–80.

Chapter 6
Development of Theoretical DERESIS Model

In this chapter, the syntheses of the methods, which are introduced in this chapter, are represented. These methods are integrated into developing the DERESIS model. The DERESIS is developed from three levels: general framework for complex work systems, generic model for complex hospital systems, and specific model for outsourcing sterile goods in hospitals.

6.1 Methods for the Intelligence Phase

The intelligence phase involves data collection, integration, pre-processing, and exploration with the aim of identifying problems or opportunities (Andrienko and Andrienko 2003). The intelligence phase deals with the problem of "Why to decide?" It includes the two aspects: "What is the problem?" and "What are the objectives?" i.e. defining the problem and determining the objectives (see Fig. 6.1).

Step 1 Problem Definition

Defining the problem is the first step in good decision making. It consists of finding, identifying, and formulating the problem that call for a decision. Defining and understanding a problem is essential before proceeding to make a decision. The accurate definition of the problem affects the steps that follow. The goal of this step is to express a problem statement which describes both the initial conditions and the desired conditions. The problem statement must, however, be concise and unambiguous material, agreed by all decision makers and support staff. It can sometimes be a long iterative process to reach agreement (Fülöp 2005; Baker et al. 2001). The procedure of problem definition is shown in Fig. 6.2.

Brainstorming is usually used as a tool to identify, analyze, and develop problems. Paulus (1998) suggest that using brainstorming in decision making would help in evaluating efficacy under different circumstance. Brainstorming research is often carried out in controlled field settings. The members are asked to provide

Q. Lin, *Analysis of Resource Management in Complex Work Systems*,
DOI 10.1007/978-981-10-2170-1_6

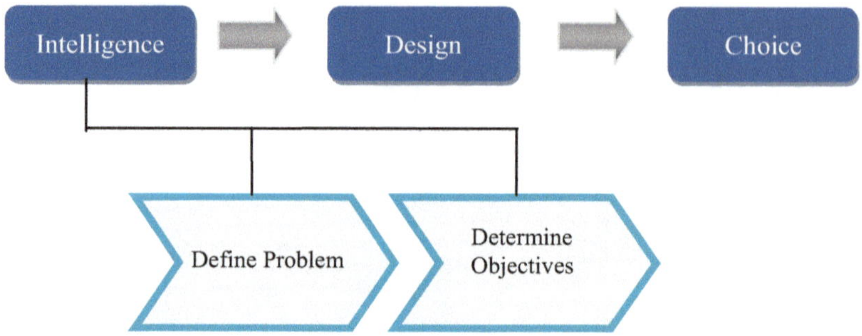

Fig. 6.1 Procedures of intelligence phase

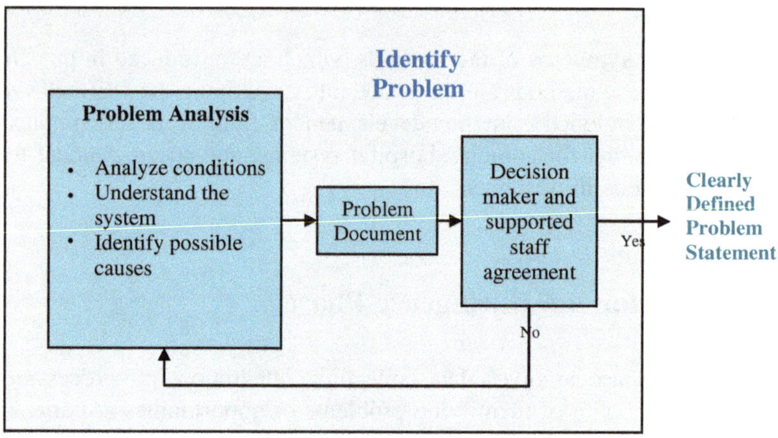

Fig. 6.2 Problem definition

innovative ideas and solutions on a topic, and to build on each other's ideas (Blumberg 2009). Creative, divergent thinking is essential in brainstorming. Using the brainstorming tool can pose enough questions about the problem to ensure that the final problem statement will answer clearly the questions of decision makers and support staff (Baker et al. 2001).

Step 2 Objectives Determination

After the definition of a problem, it is necessary to determine the objectives. It is important to understand the objectives in order to identify alternatives. The result of determining objectives is a list of objectives (see Fig. 6.3).

Fig. 6.3 Determining objectives

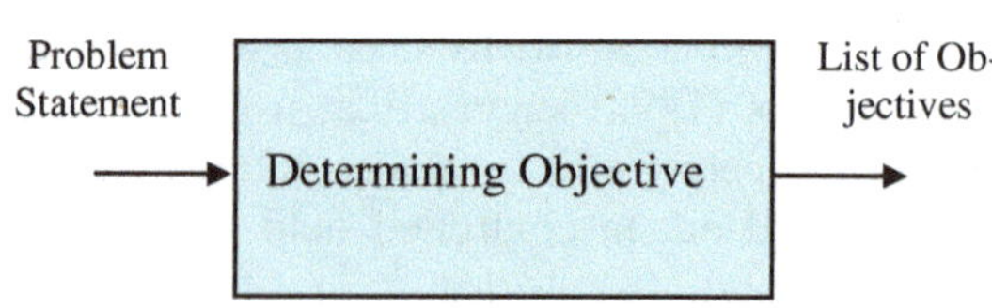

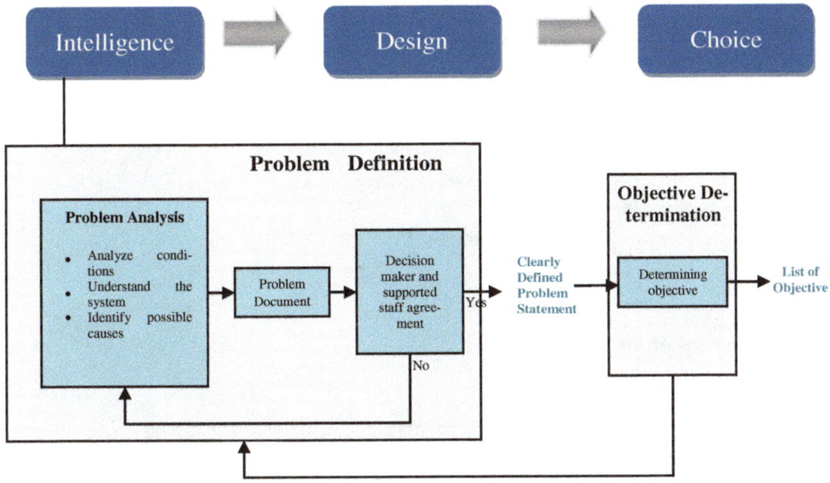

Fig. 6.4 All the procedures of the intelligence phase

Objectives are broad statements of intent and desirable values. They are useful because they can identify better alternatives. Objectives should be stated positively, and defined well, so that the pros and cons of the various alternatives considered can be thought through thoroughly.

All the procedures of the intelligence phase are depicted in Fig. 6.4.

A decision statement is the end result of the intelligence phase.

6.2 Methods for the Design Phase

After defining the problems and determining the objectives, the appropriate alternatives need to be generated (see Fig. 6.5). In the design phase, one looks for a set of possible solutions to the problems identified in the intelligence phase, and analyzes the options discovered as a result.

One of the best known methods for developing alternatives is through brainstorming, where a group works together to generate ideas and alternative solutions. The Delphi technique is another way to develop alternatives. Holistic and logical thinking to comprehend the situation, and creative skills in generating the options which fit the situation, are helpful in discovering alternative. Furthermore, knowledge of both the internal and external environments of the organizations would also help in arriving at better alternatives (Asopa and Beye 1997).

Defining alternatives occurs typically in three steps: generation, refinement, and evaluation (see Fig. 6.6). An understanding of organizational and external constraints as well as organizational resources will help to identify the range of feasible alternative actions (Asopa and Beye 1997).

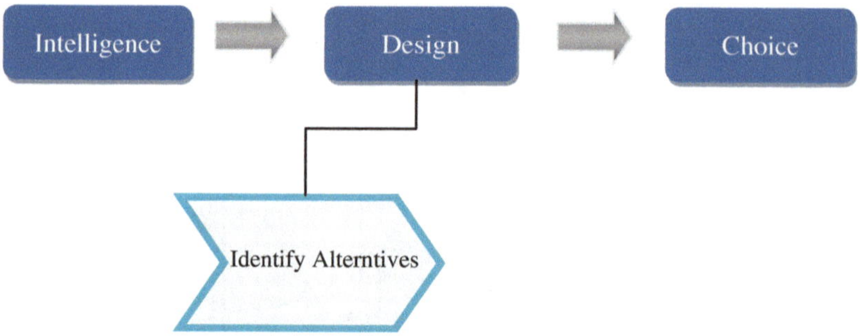

Fig. 6.5 Procedures of the design phase

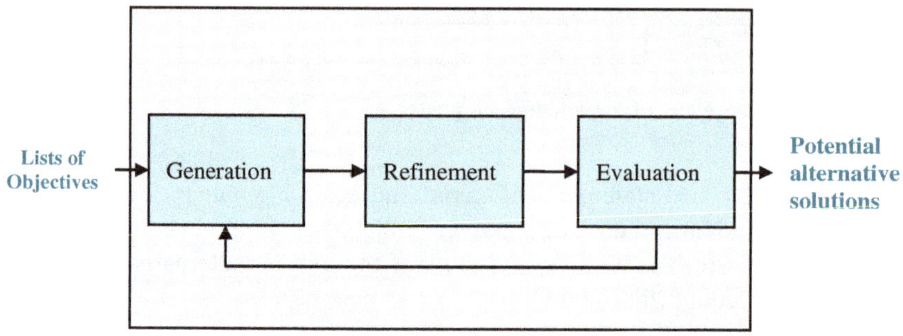

Fig. 6.6 Identification of alternatives

In the generation phase, the decision team focuses on the objectives in an effort to produce ideas on how to perform the identified function. The generation phase often results in concepts which are not feasible.

Next, in the refinement phase, the decision support team combines and completes the concepts so that they become alternatives worthy of consideration.

The last phase is evaluation. In this phase, the alternatives should be checked to see whether they meet the objectives, and whether each of them is distinct.

Alternatives must be defined to explain clearly how they will solve the particular problem. And they must be defined to enable comparative analysis. This may require a good description, and a diagram of the specific functions performed, to remedy the problem. Each definition should enable the decision team to understand how alternatives could solve the problem and how they would differ from the alternatives (Baker et al. 2001). The complete procedure for the design phase is described in Fig. 6.7.

Potential alternative solutions are the consequence of the design phase.

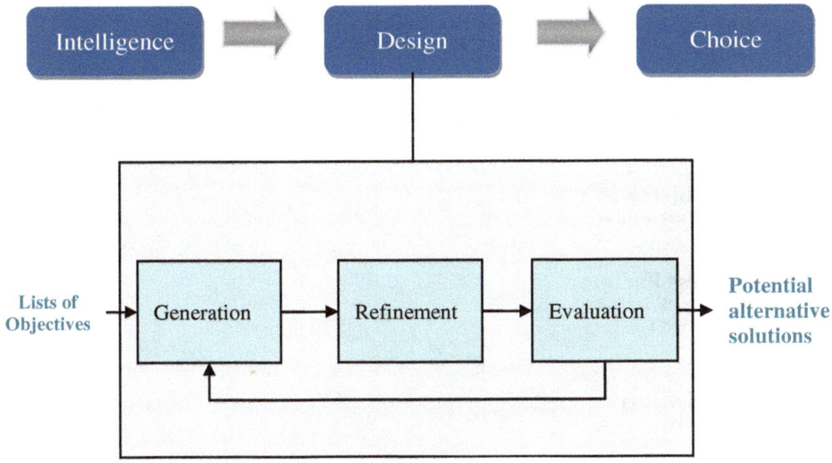

Fig. 6.7 The Complete procedures for the design phase

6.3 Methods for the Choice Phase

This phase deals with the problem of "Which alternative is best?" The organization adopts procedures involving a step-by-step process to arrive at the decision. The choice phase is subdivided into three steps:

(1) Developing a criteria system;
(2) Designing an assessment system;
(3) Selecting the best choice.

The procedures are described in Fig. 6.8.

Step 1 Develop Criteria System

In this book, a BSC was used to develop the criteria. For a complex system, it is difficult to obtain the quantitative data. Also it is insufficient to only analyze the

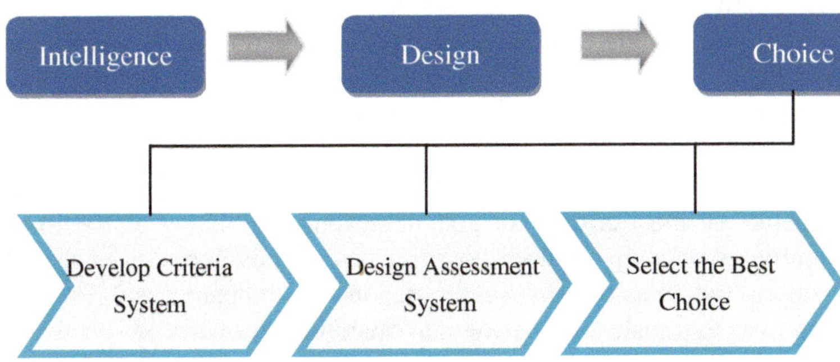

Fig. 6.8 Procedures of the choice phase

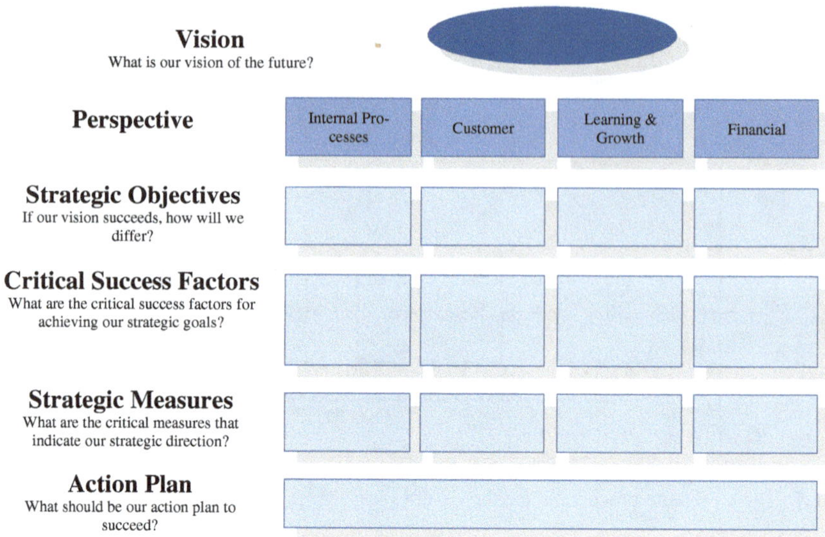

Fig. 6.9 Comprehensive view of Balanced Scorecard process. *Source* Olve et al. (1999)

quantitative criteria. So we propose BSC, which is a multidimensional measured performance for a strategic decision, in order to develop a criteria system.

The BSC will provide us with useful documentation for continually developing those control measures which will most quickly guide the company towards achieving its goals and its vision (Olve et al. 1999). The "top-down approach" is proposed to describe the process of establishing performance measures, starting with the identification and formalization of the company's vision (Biazzo and Garengo 2012). The overview of how the scorecard is developed is provided in Fig. 6.9.

The uppermost portion of the comprehensive view of BSC process is the vision at the highest level. The purposes of the vision are to guide, control, and challenge an entire organization towards realizing a shared concept of the company in the future. The overall vision is described in terms of a number of perspectives: internal processes perspective, customer perspective, learning and growth perspective, and financial perspective. The vision is expressed as a number of more specific strategic aims. They serve to guide the organization in achieving the vision. And then the factors which are most critical for the organization's success with its vision are described. Next to be described are the strategic measures which enable management to follow the organization's systematic efforts to exploit those success factors which are considered most critical for goal achievement (Olve et al. 1999).

The executive workshop is used to discuss and develop consensus of the statements about the mission and future vision of company, and to establish strategic objectives to translate the vision into operations for each perspective of the BSC (Biazzo and Garengo 2012). Since the BSC is based on a shared comprehensive vision, it is essential to ascertain vision at an early stage. Before

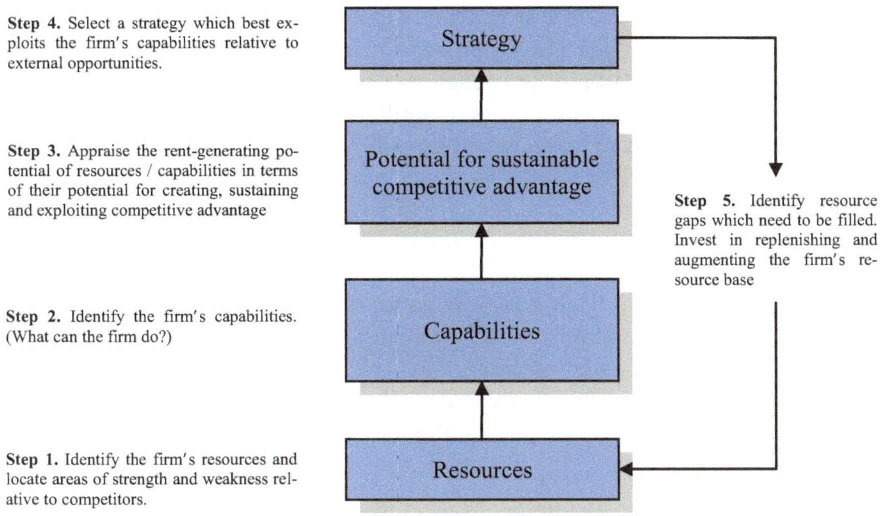

Fig. 6.10 A framework for resource analysis. *Source* Grant (1993)

establishing the vision, it is necessary firstly to define the company's current position and role. In order to develop a view of the company and its characteristics from as many angles as possible, the resource-based approach is used (see Fig. 6.10). It shifts from the external environment to the resources and capabilities of the individual company. In dealing with the external environment, a company builds its competitive power using its resources and capabilities (Olve et al. 1999).

From the resource analysis, the researcher can obtain the company's development and the current position and role. In order to establish the vision, a number of factors must be considered (see Fig. 6.11).

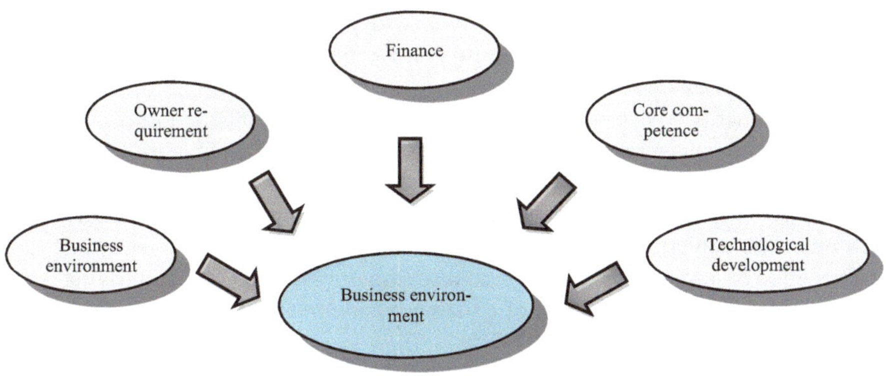

Fig. 6.11 Some factors which should be discussed, and form the basis for establishing the vision. *Source* Olve et al. (1999)

Considering the different factors can help top management to identify where the organization is going. When the vision has been established, researchers should obtain one final confirmation of how each participant perceives the vision.

In model of Kaplan and Norton, there are four perspectives: the financial, customer, internal process, and learning and growth perspectives. The development of perspectives should show the ways in which management intends to develop the organization, and the products and services offered for the purpose of streamlining processes and/or adding value for customers. This research considers the four perspectives.

After establishing the vision and formulating the strategic objectives, we must discuss and judge what is required for the vision to succeed, and which factors will have the greatest effect on the outcome.

Next, the task of translating critical success factors into performance measures is undertaken. There are some criteria which are useful in determining these measures (Olve et al. 1999):

- Measures should be unambiguous and defined uniformly throughout the company.
- Measures should cover sufficiently the aspects of the business which are included in strategies and critical success factors.
- Measures used in the different perspectives should be clearly connected. The scorecard should be interpreted as a coherent and convincing report. It should show clearly how the efforts described in the lower portion are logically justifiable to attain successfully the criteria in the upper portion.
- Measures should be useful for setting goals which are considered to be realistic by those responsible for achieving them.
- Measurement must be an easy, uncomplicated process. It must be possible to use the measurements in different systems.

The financial perspective is regularly represented by data describing the economic results of previous activities. Many traditional instruments of management control form the financial measures. Kaplan and Norton refer to three strategic themes which relate to the rate of growth and product mix; cost reduction and improved productivity; and the basic rules for capacity utilization and investment strategy (Olve et al. 1999).

The customer perspective describes the ways in which value is to be created for customers. It emphasizes customer satisfaction. The core indicators in this perspective are: market share; customer loyalty; customer satisfaction; customer acquisition; and customer profitability. The core measures and the connection to each other are depicted in following figure (see Fig. 6.12).

The internal process perspective focuses on monitoring and improving cost, quality, and time-based measures of existing business processes. The measures for this perspective are (Olve et al. 1999):

- Productivity, usually measured as quality in relation to time worked and to cost
- Quality, either the percentage of acceptable units or the opinion of some users

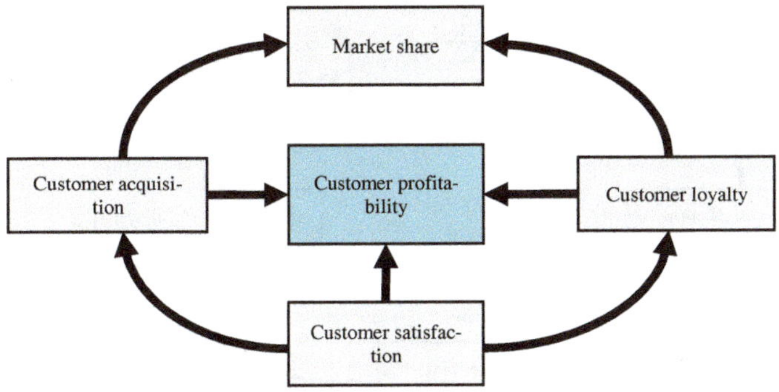

Market share	Express the extent of a business in a given market (as the number of customers, the amounts spent or sold units)
Customer ac-quisition	Measure the extent to which a business unit attracts or wins new customers (in absolute or relative terms)
Customer loy-alty	Measure the extent to which a business entity receives or gains permanent relationship with its customers.
Customer sat-isfaction	Examine the degree of satisfaction of customers based on specific performance criteria
Customer prof-itability	Measure the net profit of a customer or a segment taking into account the one-off expenditure incurred for the customer.

Fig. 6.12 The core measures from the customer perspective. *Source* Kaplan and Norton (1997)

- Level of technology compared to the most modern methods
- Capacity utilization
- Waiting queues and waiting times
- Share of resource or working time spent on the process, either within the unit concerned or as a part of a longer flow, or an entire production process.

In the learning and growth perspective, goals and metrics which promote learning and growing an organization will be developed. Investments in qualified staff and organizational learning processes are the starting point of learning and growing an organization. The learning and growth perspective stresses the importance of investing for the future. Organizations should invest in their infrastructure: people, systems, and procedures. There are three main principal categories for learning and growth perspective according to Kaplan and Norton (1997):

- Employee capabilities
- Information systems capabilities
- Motivation, empowerment, and alignment.

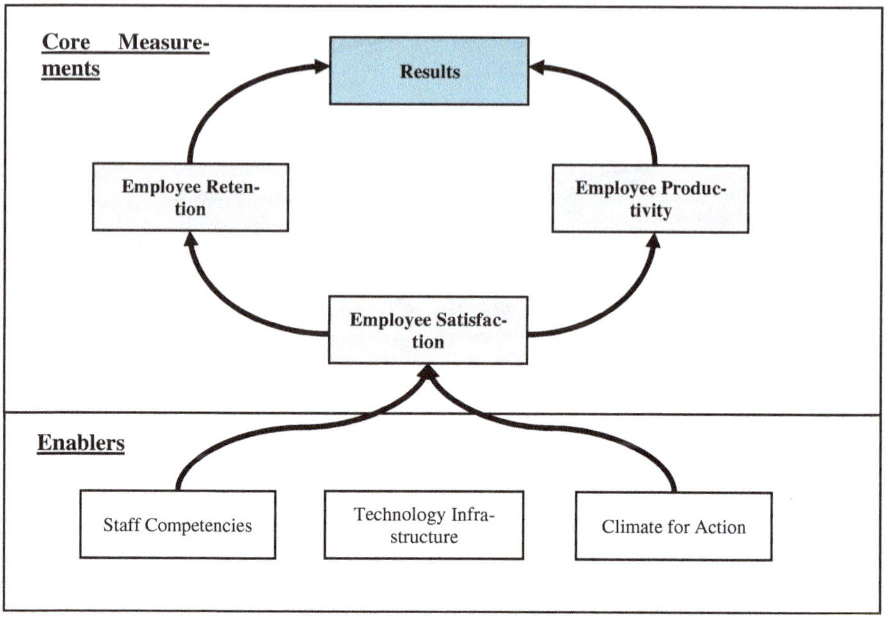

Fig. 6.13 The Framework for indicators of the learning and growth perspective. *Source* Kaplan and Norton (1996)

Most companies use employee objectives to draw from a common core of three measurements of outcomes. The core outcome measurements are supplemented with situation-specific drivers of the outcomes (see Fig. 6.13) (Kaplan and Norton 1996).

In these core measurements, the employee satisfaction objective is generally considered the driver of the other two measures, employee retention and employee productivity (Kaplan and Norton 1996). In order to choose the measures for the core employee measurement, we should firstly identify the situation-specific, unique drivers. The drivers which tend to be drawn from three critical enablers are: reskilling the work force, information systems capabilities, and motivation, empowerment, and alignment (Kaplan and Norton 1996).

After the identification of the measures for each perspective, the task is to find clear cause-and-effect relationships, and to create a balance between the different measures. The cause-and-effect relationship between strategic initiatives and measures is depicted in Fig. 6.14.

When the previous steps have been completed, we can obtain the comprehensive scorecard.

The use of the BSC method to develop a criteria system is depicted in Fig. 6.15.

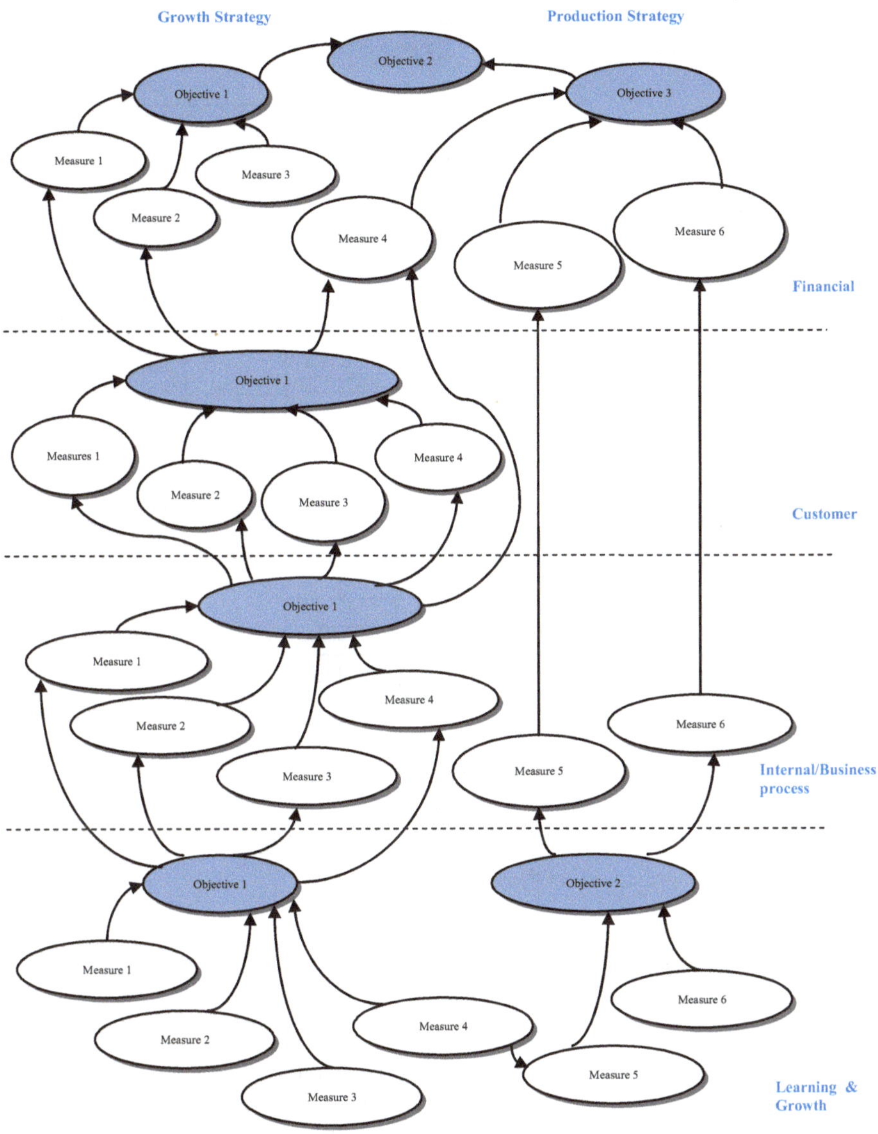

Fig. 6.14 Cause-and-effect relationships between strategic objectives and measures. *Source* Olve et al. (1999)

Step 2 Design Assessment System

After developing the criteria system, the next step is to design an assessment system. In this step, guidelines are given to help assess the alternatives, based on the various selection criteria. Fuzzy linguistic evaluation is used to assess each alternative on the selected criterion. Within the criteria system a number of qualitative

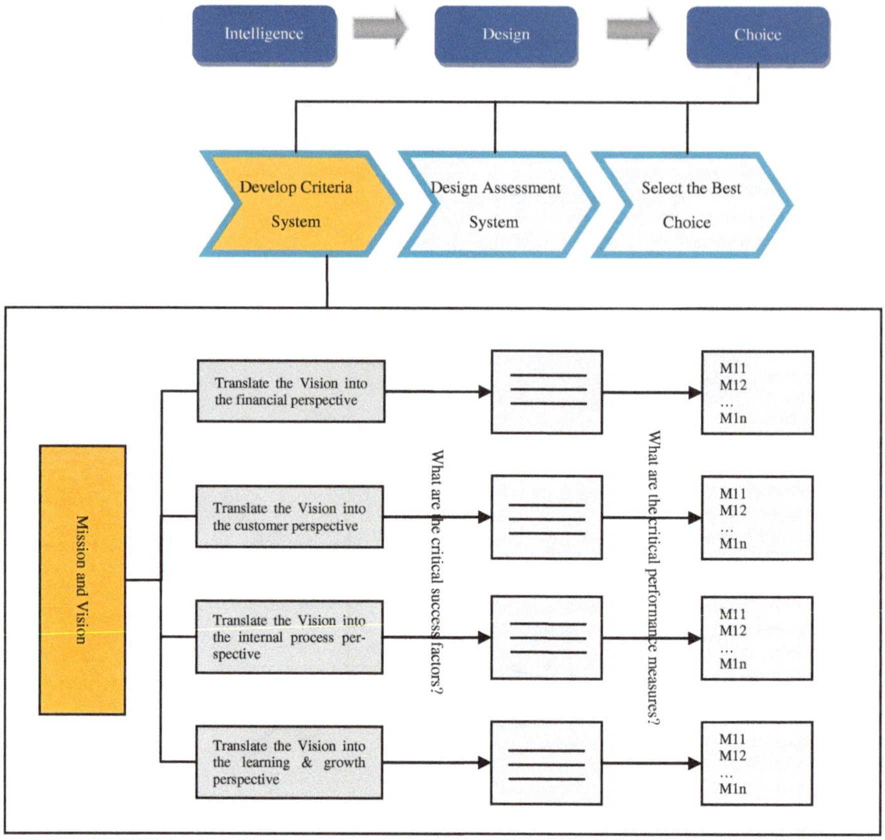

Fig. 6.15 Development of criteria in the choice phase

criteria are included, which cannot be assessed in a precise quantitative form. Thus, the use of a linguistic approach is necessary. The fuzzy linguistic evaluation is based on the expertise of the constructed group. Individual experts are asked to provide an evaluation of a predefined set of alternatives, in order to select the best one. The evaluation consists of a rating for each alternative using each of the criteria. Each of the criteria also has a different level of importance.

The group includes experts from a wide variety of expertise. We assume that each expert considers the same sets of alternatives and criteria. Since each expert has a different influence on the results, the weights of the experts must be determined. Using the 100-points moderator to define the expertise of the experts, the weights of experts are calculated by Cebi and Kahraman (2010).

$$W_{em} = \frac{P_{em}}{\sum_{m=1}^{z} P_{em}}, \quad m = 1, 2, 3, \ldots, z \tag{6.1}$$

where em and P symbolize the "Expert m" and the expertise point, respectively.

As introduced in Chap. 5, the five-scale fuzzy linguistic evaluation is used to describe the performance and importance values of the alternatives. The five scale fuzzy evaluation for the performance value of each criterion is: very poor (VP), poor (P), fair (F), good (G), and very good (VG).

VP = Very Poor = (0,0,15),
P = Poor = (10,25,40),
F = Fair = (35,50,65),
G = Good = (60,75,90),
VG = Very Good = (85,100,100).

The experts give their performance values for each criterion for the alternatives according to their own understanding. The fuzzy linguistic evaluation of the performance value of each criterion for the alternatives is shown in Fig. 6.16.

Each criterion can have a different degree of importance. Therefore, the five scale fuzzy evaluation for the importance value of each criterion is: absolutely unimportant (AU), unimportant (U), moderately important (MI), important (I), and very important (VI).

AU = Absolutely Unimportant = (0,0,0.15),
U = Unimportant = (0.1,0.25,0.40),
MI = Moderately Important = (0.35,0.5,0.65),
I = Important = (0.6,0.75,0.9),
VI = Very Important = (0.85,1,1).

Criteria			Experts				
			E1	E2	E3	...	E_k
BSC	Financial Perspective	M11					
		M12					
		...					
		M1n					
	Customer Perspective	M21					
		M22					
		...					
		M2n					
	Internal Process perspective	M31					
		M32					
		...					
		M3n					
	Learning & Growth Perspective	M41					
		M42					
		...					
		M4n					

Fuzzy linguistic evaluation

{ VP, P, F, G, VG }

Fig. 6.16 Fuzzy linguistic evaluation of the performance value of each criterion for the alternatives

Criteria			Experts				
			E1	E2	E3	…	E_k
BSC	Financial Perspective	M11					
		M12					
		…					
		M1n					
	Customer Perspective	M21					
		M22					
		…					
		M2n					
	Internal Process perspective	M31					
		M32					
		…					
		M3n					
	Learning & Growth Perspective	M41					
		M42					
		…					
		M4n					

Fuzzy linguistic evaluation

{AU, U, MI, I, VI}

Fig. 6.17 Fuzzy linguistic evaluation of the importance value of each criterion for the alternatives

Similarly, the experts give their importance value for each criterion for the alternatives according to their own understanding. The fuzzy linguistic evaluation of the importance value of each criterion for the alternatives is shown in Fig. 6.17.

Fuzzy linguistic evaluation is based on the use of the linguistic approach, and it is applied to solving decision making problems using linguistic information. It is beneficial for decision analysis because it introduces a more flexible framework, which allows us to represent the information in a more direct and adequate way when we are unable to express it precisely (Herrera and Herrera-Viedma 2000). Using fuzzy linguistic evaluation for the design assessment system is depicted in Fig. 6.18.

Step 3 Select the Best Choice

The last step of the choice phase is selecting the best choice. After the fuzzy linguistic evaluation, we get the fuzzy linguistic number. It is difficult to compare the fuzzy linguistic number to get the best choice. Therefore, in order to get the non-fuzzy value, we propose the defuzzification procedure to convert the fuzzy result into a numerical value. The defuzzification methods for the performance value and importance value of each criterion on the alternatives are shown below.

$$\mathrm{DP}_{ij}^{m} = \frac{\left[\left(\mathrm{UP}_{ij}^{m} - \mathrm{LP}_{ij}^{m}\right) + \left(\mathrm{MP}_{ij}^{m} - \mathrm{LP}_{ij}^{m}\right)\right]}{3} + \mathrm{LP}_{ij}^{m}\ \forall i \tag{6.2}$$

$$\mathrm{DI}_{ij}^{m} = \frac{\left[\left(\mathrm{UI}_{ij}^{m} - \mathrm{LI}_{ij}^{m}\right) + \left(\mathrm{MI}_{ij}^{m} - \mathrm{LI}_{ij}^{m}\right)\right]}{3} + \mathrm{LI}_{ij}^{m}\ \forall i \tag{6.3}$$

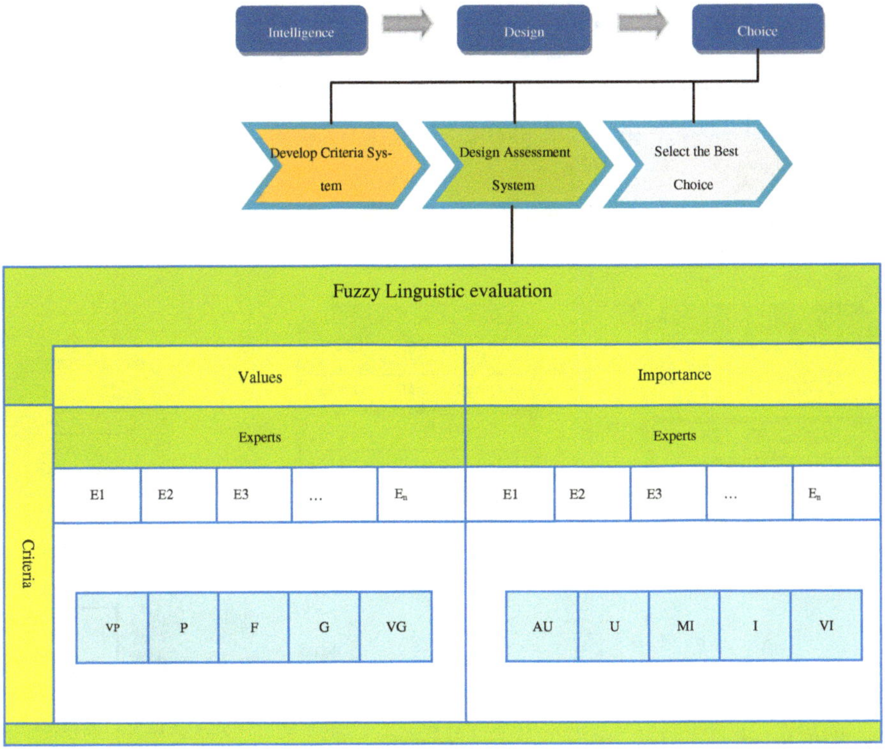

Fig. 6.18 Assessment system in the choice phase

After the defuzzification, we can obtain the non-fuzzy value of an expert for each criterion for the alternatives. As the evaluation is based on expertise, we must consider the weight of experts. Therefore, the aggregation of the experts' values for performance and importance are:

$$DP_{ij} = DP^1_{ij} * W_{e1} + DP^2_{ij} * W_{e2} + \cdots + DP^m_{ij} * W_{em} \tag{6.4}$$

$$DI_{ij} = DI^1_{ij} * W_{e1} + DI^2_{ij} * W_{e2} + \cdots + DI^m_{ij} * W_{em} \tag{6.5}$$

DS is the score of evaluation of the alternatives against the criteria. The DS is calculated with DP_{ij} and DI_{ij}.

$$DS = \sum DP_{ij} * DI_{ij} \tag{6.6}$$

After the evaluation, the alternatives can be ranked according to the value of DS. The maximum value of DS is the best choice.

The detailed procedures of step 3 selecting the best choice are shown in Fig. 6.19.

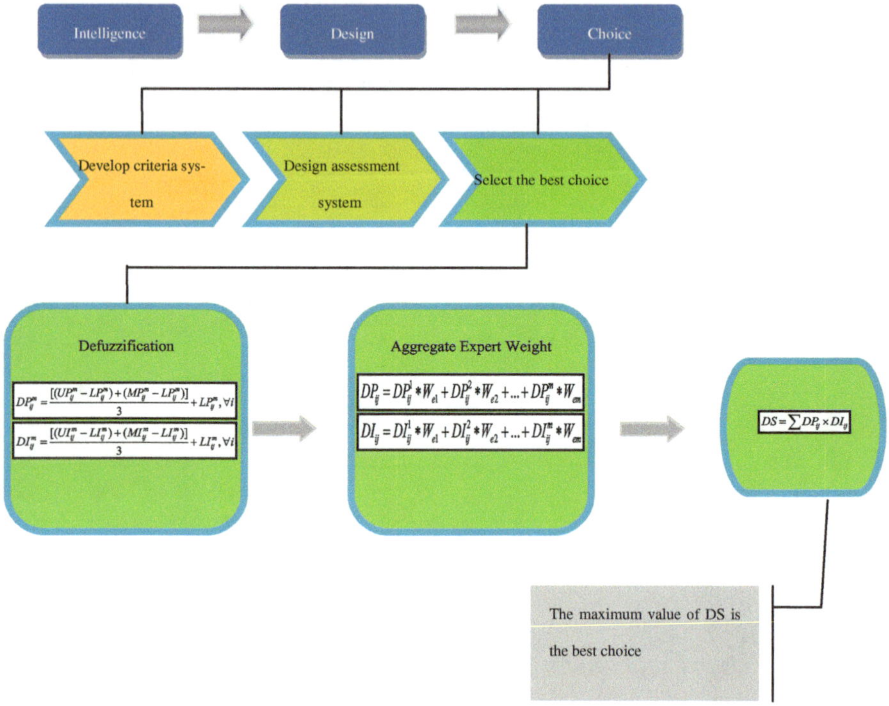

Fig. 6.19 Selecting the best choice in the choice phase

The choice phase proposes methods to evaluate, rate, and compare different alternatives, which are developed in the design phase. It describes the acceptability of a solution approach. In the choice phase, it deals with the problems of "What criteria are used to decide?", "Who participates in determining and evaluating the criteria?", "How is the evaluation done", and "Which is the best one". The end product of this phase is a decision.

All the procedures of the choice phase are depicted in Fig. 6.20.

6.4 DERESIS Model

6.4.1 General Framework

There are three main different stages in DERESIS: intelligence, design, and choice. "Why decide?" is dealt with in the intelligence phase. "What are the alternatives?" is considered in the design phase. The last phase—the choice phase, considers "Which alternative is best?" Based on the Simon decision making model, we proposed the general framework of DERESIS. Figure 6.21 shows how we started

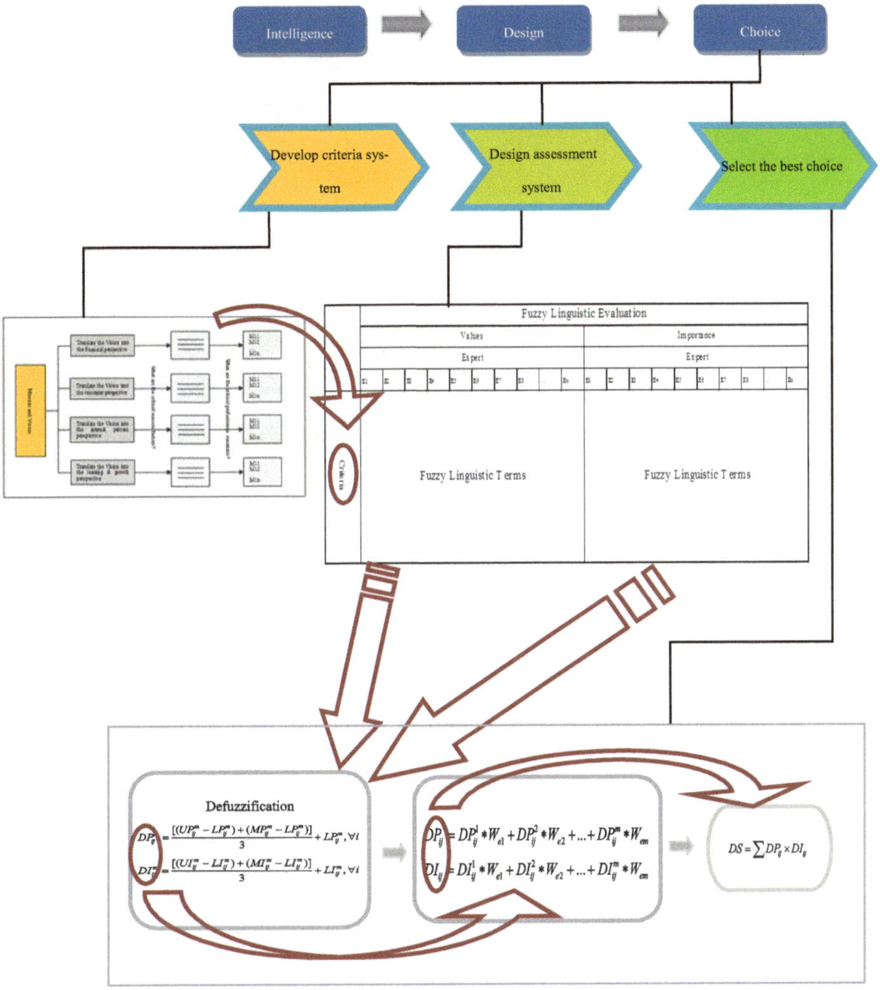

Fig. 6.20 All the procedures of the choice phase

with Simon's three stage model, and then adapted it to six stages to better reflect DERESIS.

Generally speaking, intelligence activity precedes design, and design activity precedes choice. However, the phases form a cycle. The cycle is far more complex than this sequence suggests. Each phase in making a particular decision is itself a complex decision making process. The design phase may call for new intelligence activities. The choice phase may call for new intelligence activities and design activities. Problems at any given level generate sub-problems that, in turn, have their intelligence, design, and choice phases, and so on (Simon 1960). The relationship of the six stages of the DERESIS model is described in Fig. 6.22.

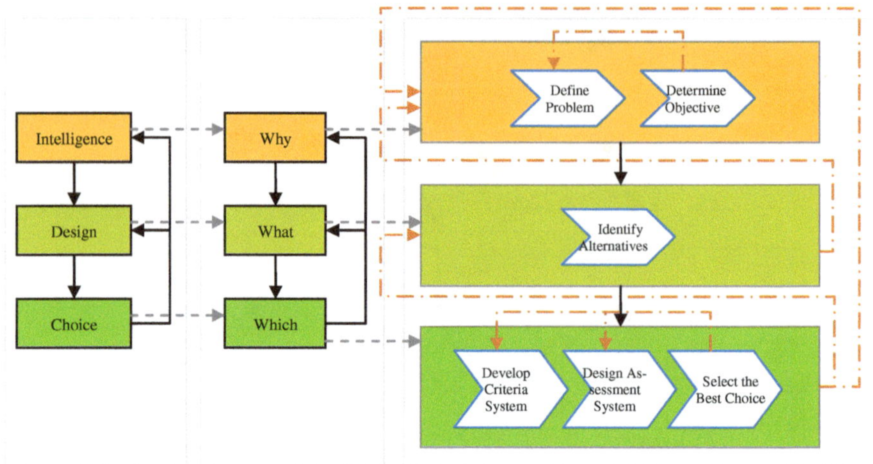

Fig. 6.21 General framework of DERESIS

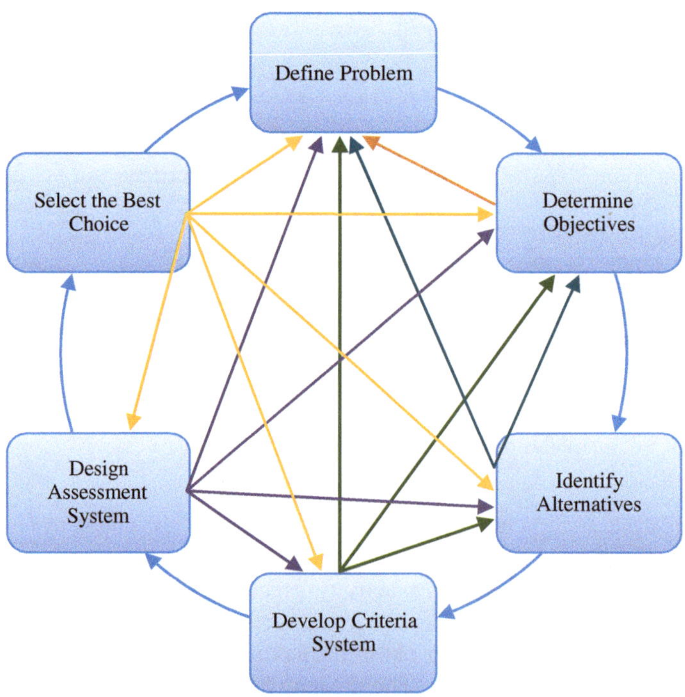

Fig. 6.22 Relationship of the six stages of DERESIS model

In a complex work system, the decision making process is very complicated. It is not treated in a linear manner. However, it is necessary to deal with it in an iterative and networked process. For example, in identification of alternatives stage, it is necessary to return to the problem definition and objectives determination in order to obtain more information or reconsider strategies. Because there are numerous components and interconnections in a complex work system, the situation will change both continuously and discontinuously. The complex systems have high variety and are highly networked.

6.4.2 Generic Model

The decision making model for resource management of complex work systems is based on the three main stages model: intelligence phase, design phase, and choice phase. In each phase, there are some sub-phases. In the intelligence phase, there are two sub-phases: problem definition and objectives determination. In the design phase, the main task is to identify the alternatives. And in the choice phase, there are three steps to reach the best alternative: criteria system development, assessment system design, and selecting the best choice. For decision making in a complex work system, there are so many interconnections between each phase, the process is not a linear one but an iterative and networked process. It is necessary to return to previous steps to obtain more information and reconsider strategies.

For each phase, we use the input and output model to carry out the procedures. The input-process-output model with feedback is described in Fig. 6.23.

There is an input and output in each phase/step, but the output does not mean the end of the process and the gaining of a result. Because of the variety, interconnection, and dynamism between components in a complex work system, it is more complicated and it is necessary to return to the input in order to reconsider the situation.

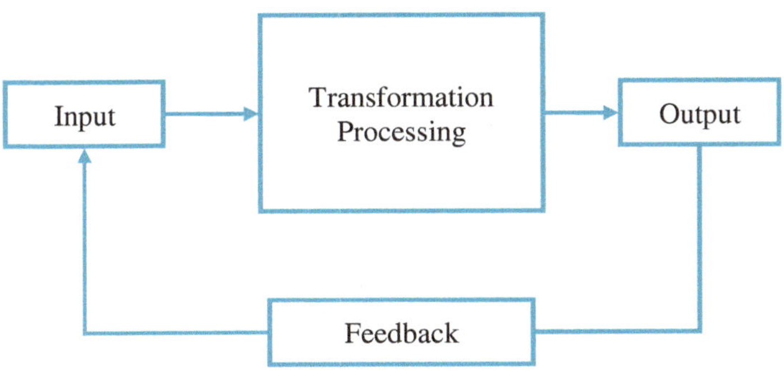

Fig. 6.23 The input-process-output model

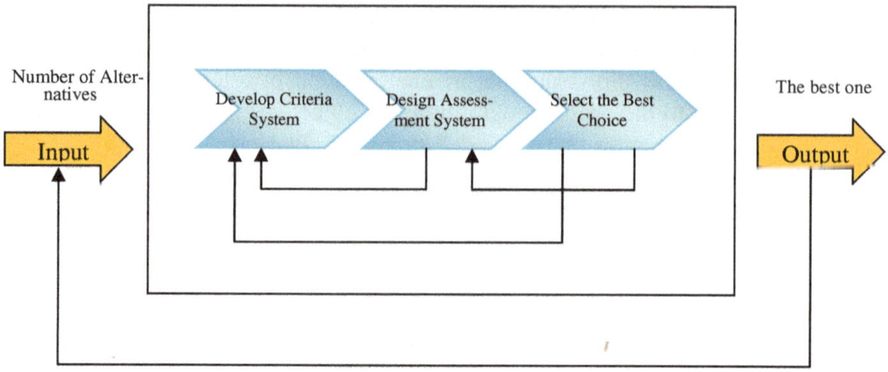

Fig. 6.24 The input-process-output in the choice phase

Brainstorming is usually used to identify, analyze, and develop problems, and is also the tool need to develop alternatives for solving problems. After the analysis of the first two phases, we can obtain a number of alternatives for decision making. These alternatives are the input of the choice phase and using the choice phase processes we reach the output: which is the best choice. In the complex work system the output is not the end result of the decision making process. It is necessary to return to the previous phase to check if the choice is in accord with the objectives, and if it solves the current problems. This is because the situation is always changing in complex work systems. The input-process-output for the choice phase is shown in Fig. 6.24.

In this book, we use BSC to develop the criteria system, and fuzzy linguistic evaluation to design the assessment system for decision making in complex hospital systems. In a complex hospital system it is difficult to obtain the quantitative data, and it requires more quantitative criteria and fuzzy assessment for the decision making. The BSC and fuzzy linguistic evaluation are based on the expertise of the constructed group. The interaction between multiple parties, subject to manifold psychological, social, and contextual influences, is one of the most difficult topics of study in the human sciences (Poole and Hirokawa 1996). Group communication is important for decision making. Communication within a group is a necessary precondition for high-quality group decision making. Therefore, more attention must be paid to communication within the group through all the procedures of DERESIS. All the procedures of the generic model of DERESIS are depicted in Fig. 6.25.

6.4.3 *Specific Model*

The decision making model for the sterile goods management in hospitals is the specific model of the DERESIS. Sterile goods are vitally important for the surgical

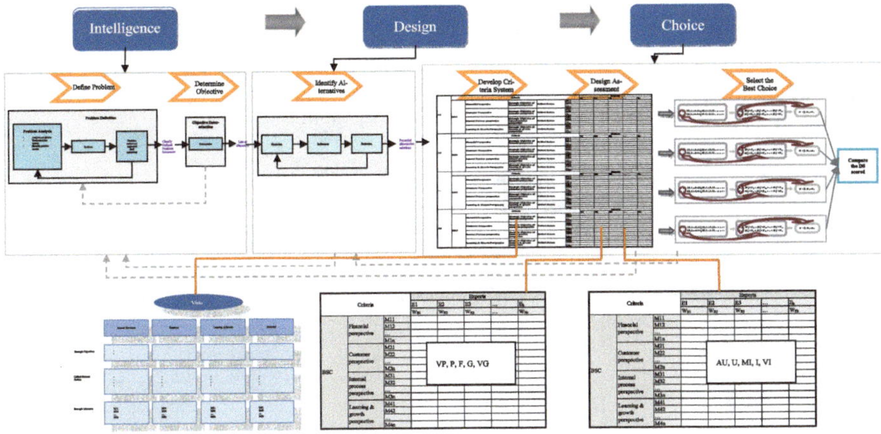

Fig. 6.25 The generic model of DERESIS

department. Defects in sterile goods supply can lead to catastrophic consequences. The management of sterile goods in hospital is becoming more important in hospital management.

Currently, most hospitals have their own CSSD for sterile goods. It means that hospitals have in-house sterile goods. But considering the high opportunity cost of CSSD, many hospital managers pay more attention to outsourcing the CSSD.

Considering the previously mentioned methods the DERESIS model is proposed for sterile goods management. This model is also based on the three main phases of the decision making model: intelligence, design, and choice phase. In each phase there are some steps. Following the six steps in the model, we can reach a decision. In this specific model for sterile goods management, we consider the in-house or outsourcing of sterile goods. There are therefore only two alternatives for a decision: in-house and outsourcing. The main task is to decide which (in-house or outsourcing) is better for hospital development. A criteria system must be developed to compare the two alternatives. The BSC is used to develop the criteria system for hospital development. In the development process, workshops are held to explain the mission, core values and vision and to determine strategic objectives, initiatives, and indicators in order to implement a system for the BSC executive team to monitor.

A hospital is a complex work system. It also involves a large number of inter-connection and the behavior of the system is dynamic. Therefore, in the decision making process for sterile goods, the best choice which we reach first is not the result of research. It is also necessary to return to the previous step to check if it is in accord with the objectives and if it solves the current problems.

All the procedures of the specific model of DERESIS are depicted Fig. 6.26.

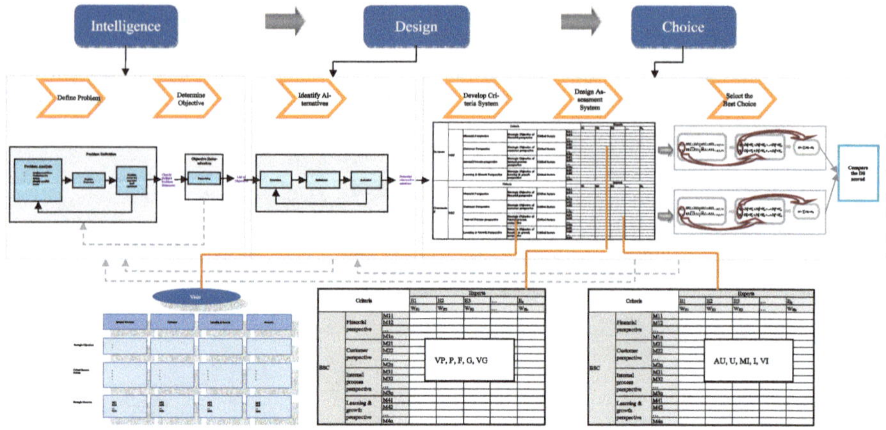

Fig. 6.26 The specific model of DERESIS

References

Andrienko, N., & Andrienko, G. (2003). *Informed spatial decision making using coordinated views*. Retrieved June 16, 2013, from http://geoanalytics.net/and/papers/ivs03.pdf

Asopa, V. N., & Beye, G. (1997). Management of agricultural research: A training manual. *Introduction Module*. Retrieved May 21, 2013, from http://www.fao.org/docrep/W7500E/W7500E00.htm

Baker, D., Bridges, D., Hunter, R., Johnson, G., Krupa, J., Murphy, J., et al. (2001). *Guidebook to decision making methods*. Retrieved January 11, 2013, from http://kscsma.ksc.nasa.gov/Reliability/Documents/Decision_Making_Guidebook_2002_Dept_of_Energy.phd

Biazzo, S., & Garengo, P. (2012). The balanced scorecard for SMEs: A circular approach. In S. Biazzo & P. Garengo (Eds.), *Performance measurement with the balanced scorecard: A practical approach to implementation within SMEs*. Berlin, Heidelberg: Springer.

Blumberg, H. H. (2009). Group decision making. In H. H. Blumberg, A. P. Hare, M. V. Kent, & M. F. Davies (Eds.), *Small group research*. Bern: Peter Lang AG.

Cebi, S., & Kahraman, C. (2010). Developing a group decision support system based on fuzzy information axiom. *Knowledge-Based System, 23*(1), 3–16.

Fülöp, J. (2005). *Introduction to decision making methods*. Washington: BEDI-3 Workshop. Retrieved May 3, 2013, from http://citeseerx.ist.psu.edu/viewdoc/download?doi=10.1.1.86.6292&rep=rep1&type=pdf

Herrera, F., & Herrera-Viedma, E. (2000). Linguistic decision analysis: Steps for solving decision problems under linguistic information. *Fuzzy Sets and Systems, 115*, 67–82.

Grant, R. M. (1993). *Contemporary strategy analysis*. Oxford: Blackwell Business.

Kaplan, R. S., & Norton, D. P. (1996). *The balanced scorecard: Translating strategy into action*. Boston: Harvard Business School Press.

Kaplan, R. S., & Norton, D. P. (1997). Balanced scorecard: Strategien erfolgreich umsetzen, aus dem amerikanischen übersetzt von Horvath, P., Kuhn-Würfel, B. & Vogelhuber, C. Stuttgart: Schäffer-Poeschel Verlag.

Olve, N. G., Roy, J., & Wetter, M. (1999). *Performance drivers: A practical guide to using the balanced scorecard*. Chichester: Wiley.

Paulus, P. B. (1998). Developing consensus about groupthink after all these years. *Organizational Behavior and Human Decision Processes, 73*, 362–374.

Poole, M. S., & Hirokawa, R. Y. (1996). Introduction communication and group decision making. In R. Y. Hirokawa & M. S. Poole (Eds.), *Commnication and group decision making* (2nd ed.). California: Sage Publications.

Simon, H. A. (1960). *The new science of management decision*. New York: Harper & Brothers Publishers.

Chapter 7
Evaluation of the DERESIS Model

The evaluation of the developed model DERESIS is undertaken. The evaluation is necessary to clarify, (1) whether the developed model is suitable for deciding whether to outsource sterile goods in a hospital; (2) whether and to what extent the developed model can be implemented realistically. Firstly, it describes how the evaluation was carried out in this work. Then, a case study is used to verify the developed model. Then, the evaluation of the results is presented.

7.1 Procedure for Evaluation

In the evaluation of the developed model, the iterative relationship of the decision making process in a complex work system is verified first of all (see Fig. 7.1). As the situation changes both continuously and discontinuously in a complex work system, the decision making process is not linear. It is more complicated.

The evaluation with a case study is presented. The feasibility of the model can be checked using the example of outsourcing the sterile goods department in a hospital. The result will show whether the developed model is suitable, and whether it can be implemented realistically.

A hospital which has an in-house sterile goods department is considering outsourcing sterile goods. However, it is not know how to make a decision. So we use the previously developed model, i.e. DERESIS specific model, to make a decision. The situation of the sterile goods department in a hospital will be entered into the model. The course of the evaluation is shown in Fig. 7.2.

The evaluation is carried out in a hospital, using the expertise of the constructed group. Workshops are held to explain the problems, the BSC measures, and the fuzzy evaluation of in-house and outsourcing alternatives.

Q. Lin, *Analysis of Resource Management in Complex Work Systems*,
DOI 10.1007/978-981-10-2170-1_7

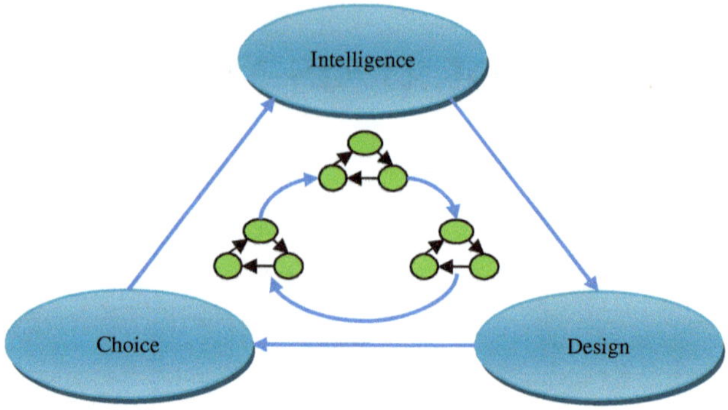

Fig. 7.1 The iterative relationship of the decision making process

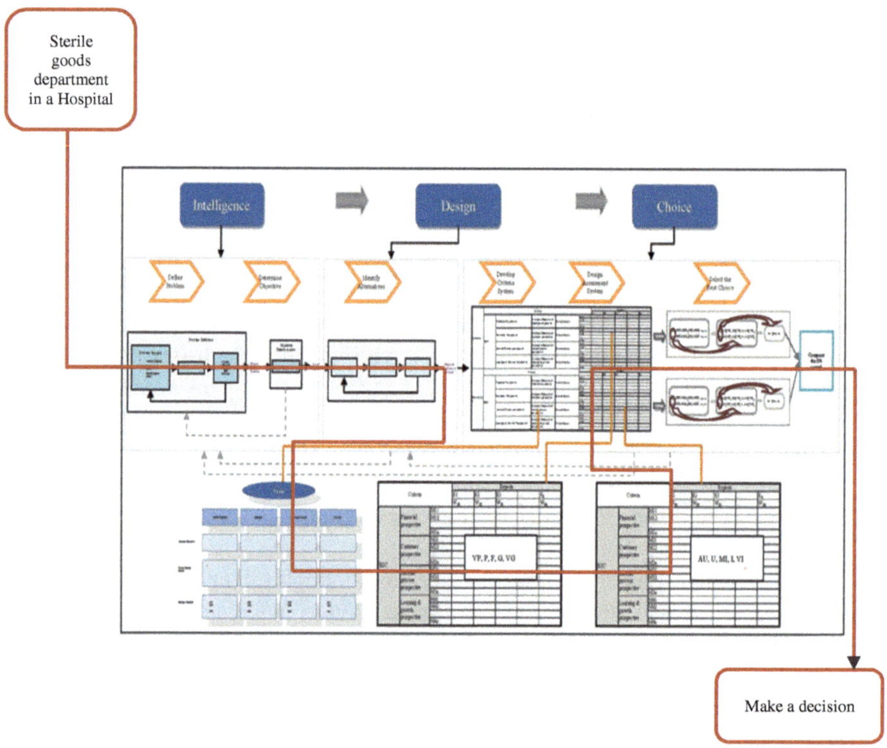

Fig. 7.2 Course of the execution with a particular sterile goods department in a hospital

7.2 Evaluation of Results

7.2.1 Evaluation of the Iterative Relationship

The model is based on the Simon's three phases of the traditional decision making process, and then the six steps of a decision making process in the DERESIS model are proposed.

The evaluation of the iterative relationship of the decision making process can proceed in two ways. One way is the iterative relationship of the three main phases' decision making. The other is the iterative relationship of six steps decision making (see Fig. 7.3).

The iterative relationship in a complex work system is very important, because of its variety and dynamism. For example, in the assessment system design step in choice phase, it must not only return to the criteria system development step, but also reconsider the alternative, and the problem and objectives steps.

7.2.2 Evaluation Using the Example

The feasibility of the model can be checked by using the example of decision making for outsourcing sterile goods in a hospital, which is located in Guangdong

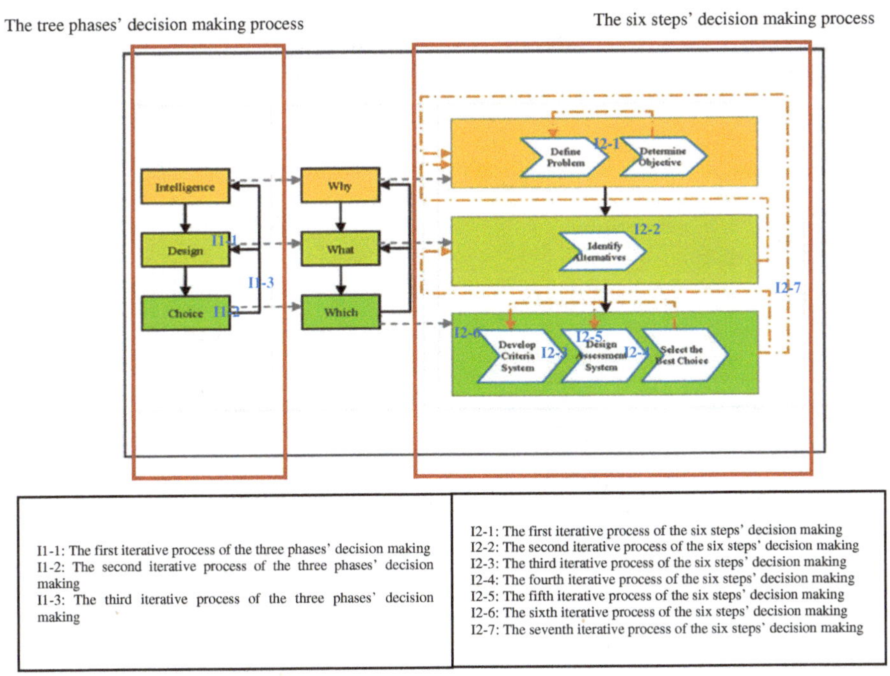

Fig. 7.3 Evaluation of the iterative relationship for the decision making process

province in China. The hospital is a general hospital. Now there are 4986 hospital staffs including 3927 medical staffs and 646 staffs with senior professional titles. The hospital has more than 2500 opening beds and the annual number of discharge was 93,000 in 2012. The number of outpatients in 2012 amounted to more than 4,110,000 (GGH 2011).

The hospital has an in-house CSSD, which services all hospital areas, including the operating suite. In consideration of the high cost and the important space in hospital, the managers want to make a decision whether or not to outsource the sterile goods. They want to know which is better for hospital development.

In Chap. 6 we introduced the three phases of the decision making process. For decision making of outsourcing sterile goods, there are two alternatives: in-house and outsourcing. In this book, we evaluate the three main parts: the criteria system development, the assessment system design, and the best choice selection (see Fig. 7.4).

Criteria System of Decision Making for Outsourcing Sterile Goods in a Hospital

The BSC is used to develop the criteria system. Workshops are held in the hospital to explain the mission, core values and vision, and to determine strategic objectives, and measures. The vision of the BSC in a hospital is to improve the efficiency and effectiveness of the service. The strategic objectives and measures of each perspective are described below.

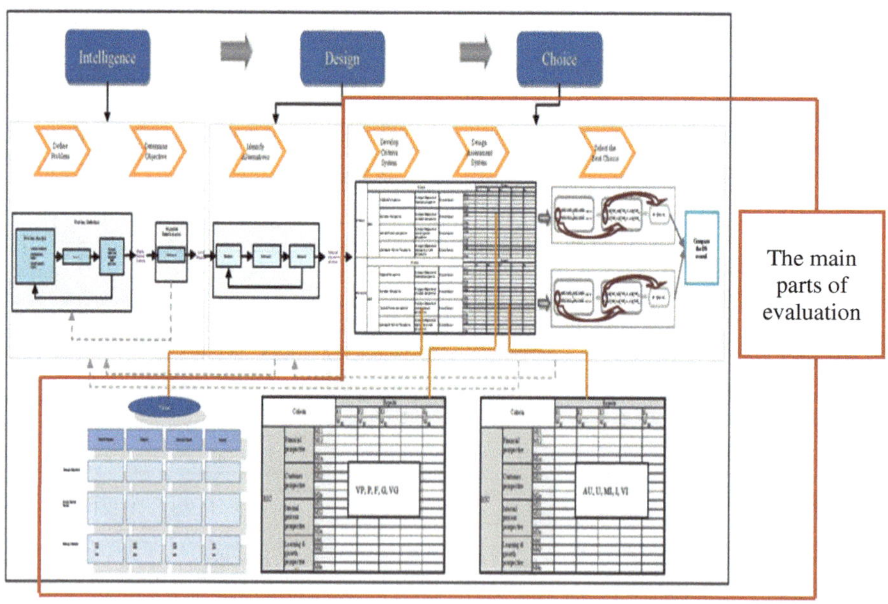

Fig. 7.4 The main evaluation parts

Developing Measures from the Financial Perspective

The financial objectives are focused on the financial long-term viability of hospitals. Financial measures are crucial in order to guarantee the efficiency of future operations. In particular, the strategic objectives of the financial perspectives include the following:

- Cost reduction of services
- Reduction of operating expenses.

The measures in this perspective are shown in Table 7.1.

Developing the Measures from the Customer Perspective

Regarding the customer perspective, the strategic objectives of the organization refer mostly to the satisfaction of multiple customers. It describes the ways in which value is to be created for multiple customers. The strategic objectives in this perspective are:

- Satisfaction of multiple customers
- Attraction of more customers.

The measures from the customer perspective are proposed in Table 7.2.

Developing Measures from the Internal Process Perspective

Quality and efficiency are not usually competitive in healthcare organizations (Shimshak et al. 2009). From the internal perspective, there is a focuses on

Table 7.1 The measures from the financial perspective

Perspective	Strategic objectives	Measures	
Financial perspective	Cost reduction of services	Low administration cost	M11
		Low distribution cost	M12
		Profit margin	M13
		Cost per employee	M14
	Reduction of operating expenses	Operating expenses	M15
		Operating revenues	M16

Table 7.2 The measures from the customer perspective

Perspective	Strategic objectives	Measures	
Customer perspective	Satisfaction of multiple customers	Effectiveness of service	M21
		Customer complaints	M22
		Waiting time for service	M23
	Attraction of customers	Customer loyalty	M24
		Customer acquisition	M25
		Market share	M26

Table 7.3 The measures from the internal process perspective

Perspective	Strategic objectives	Measures	
Internal process perspective	Efficient internal process	Continuous process improvement capability	M31
		Process standardization capability	M32
		Response when discovering mistakes	M33
		Efficient distribution system	M34
	Effective resource utilization	Human resource utilization	M35
		Facility resource utilization	M36

monitoring and improving the quality and efficiency of internal processes. The strategic objectives in this perspective are:

- Efficient internal processes
- Effective resource utilization.

Measures from the internal process perspective allow the manager to know how well their business is running, and whether its products and services conform to customer requirements. Based on the strategic objectives, the measures from the learning and growth perspective are shown in Table 7.3.

Developing Measures from the Learning and Growth Perspective

Finally, the learning and growth perspective includes strategic objectives, orientated mostly towards to the learning and growing organization, which has the ability to adopt new technology, and to respond effectively in a rapidly changing environment. In particular, the strategic objectives in learning and growth perspective are:

- High employee capabilities
- High information system capabilities
- Effective organization climate
- Third-party collaboration.

According to the strategic objective, we can obtain the measures from the learning and growth perspective (see Table 7.4).

After the four dimensions of BSC, we can obtain the overall criteria system. The overall BSC criteria system is described in Table 7.5.

In order to analyze the relationships between the different measures in the four dimensions, and to create a balance, we describe the cause-and-effect relationship between the measures. The cause-and-effect relationship between strategic objectives and measures is depicted Fig. 7.5.

Assessment System of Decision Making for Outsourcing Sterile Goods in a Hospital

Based on the criteria system of hospital development, we will assess the two alternatives, i.e. in-house and outsourcing, and which is better for the hospital

Table 7.4 The measures from the learning and growth perspective

Perspective	Strategic objectives	Measures	
Learning and growth perspective	High employee capabilities	Employee productivity	M41
		Employee satisfaction	M42
		Employee retention	M43
	High information system capabilities	The extent of information application	M44
	Effective organization climate	Internal and external communication	M45
		Collaboration within work teams	M46
		Knowledge management	M47
	Third-party collaboration	The ability to work with other organizations	M48

development. The assessment system design was introduced in Chap. 6. The application of BSC criteria to develop the fuzzy evaluation is shown in Fig. 7.6.

The fuzzy evaluation experts include hospital managers (directors of OR and CSSD, director of hospital), clinical staff (staff in OR and CSSD) and academic. There are seven experts in the workshop to assess the two alternatives, i.e. in-house and outsourcing. Because the experts have a different influence on the results, the weights of the experts should be determined. According to Eq. (5.1), the weight of experts is shown in Table 7.6.

The fuzzy numbers of the five linguistic scales for the performance value in hospital of the two alternatives are VP, P, F, G, and VG. The weight of importance of the five-scale fuzzy linguistic are AU, U, MI, I, and VI. The experts give their own opinions for the performance values and the weight of importance. Based on these expert opinions, the fuzzy linguistic of performance values in hospital of the in-house and outsourcing, and the weight of importance for each criterion are obtained (see Appendix 1 and Appendix 2).

After obtaining the expert opinions for the performance and the weight of importance, we change the expert fuzzy linguistic into a five scale fuzzy number (see Appendix 3 and Appendix 4). Equations (6.8–6.9) are then used to convert the fuzzy number into non-fuzzy values.

The non-fuzzy values of the five-scale fuzzy linguistic for the performance values in hospital are:

VP = Very Poor = (0,0,15) = 5,
P = Poor = (10,25,40) = 25,
F = Fair = (35,50,65) = 50,
G = Good = (60,75,90) = 75,
VG = Very Good = (85,100,100) = 95.

Table 7.5 The overall BSC criteria system

Vision	Perspectives	Strategic objectives	Measures
To become a general hospital to improve the efficiency and effectiveness of the service	Financial	Cost reduction of services	Low administration cost
			Low distribution cost
			Profit margin
			Cost per employee
		Reduction of operating expenses	Operating expenses
			Operating revenues
	Customer	Satisfaction of multiple customers	Effectiveness of service
			Customer complaints
			Waiting time for service
		Attraction of customers	Customer loyalty
			Customer acquisition
			Market share
	Internal process	Efficient internal process	Continuous process improvement capability
			Process standardization capability
			Response when discovering mistakes
			Efficient distribution system
		Effective resource utilization	Human resource utilization
			Facility resource utilization
	Learning and growth	High employee capabilities	Employee productivity
			Employee satisfaction
			Employee retention
		High information system capabilities	The extent of information application
		Effective organization climate	Internal and external communication
			Collaboration within work teams
			Knowledge management
		Third-party collaboration	The ability to work with other organizations

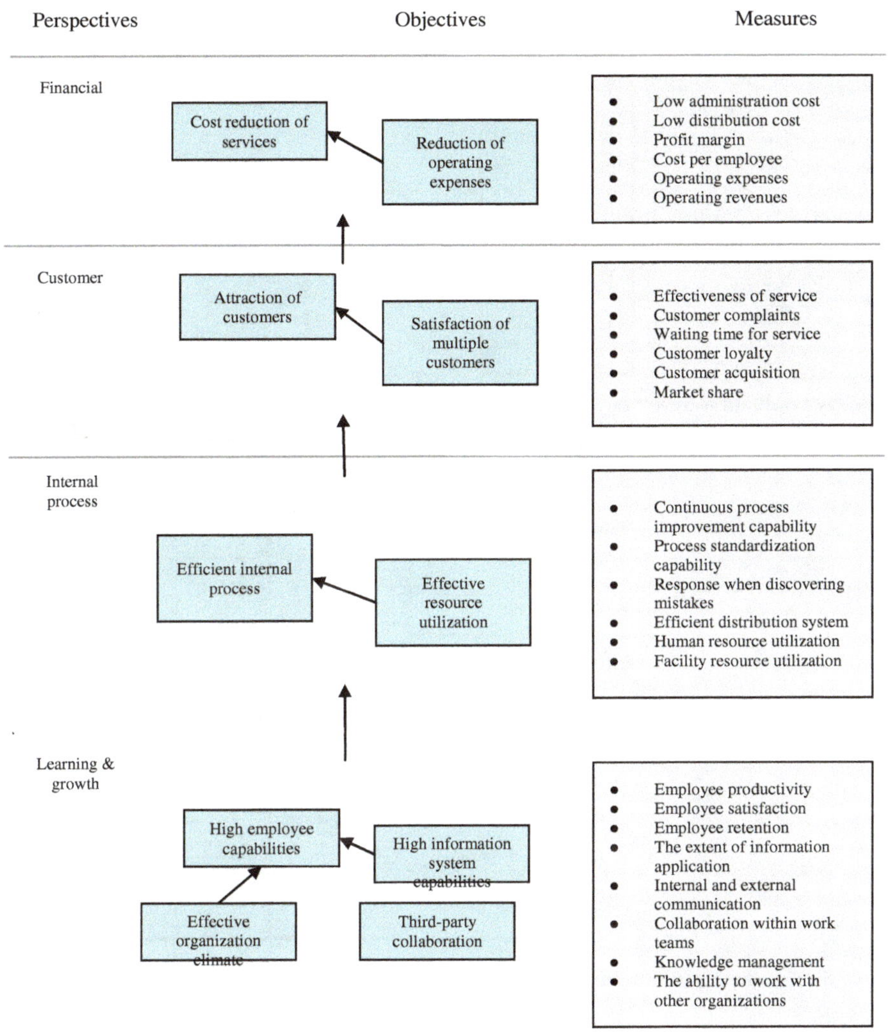

Fig. 7.5 The cause-and-effect relationship between strategic objectives and measures

And the non-fuzzy values of the five-scale for the weight of importance of each criterion are:

AU = Absolutely Unimportant = (0,0,0.15) = 0.05,
U = Unimportant = (0.1,0.25,0.40) = 0.25,
MI = Moderately Important = (0.35,0.5,0.65) = 0.5,
I = Important = (0.6,0.75,0.9) = 0.75,
VI = Very Important = (0.85,1,1) = 0.95.

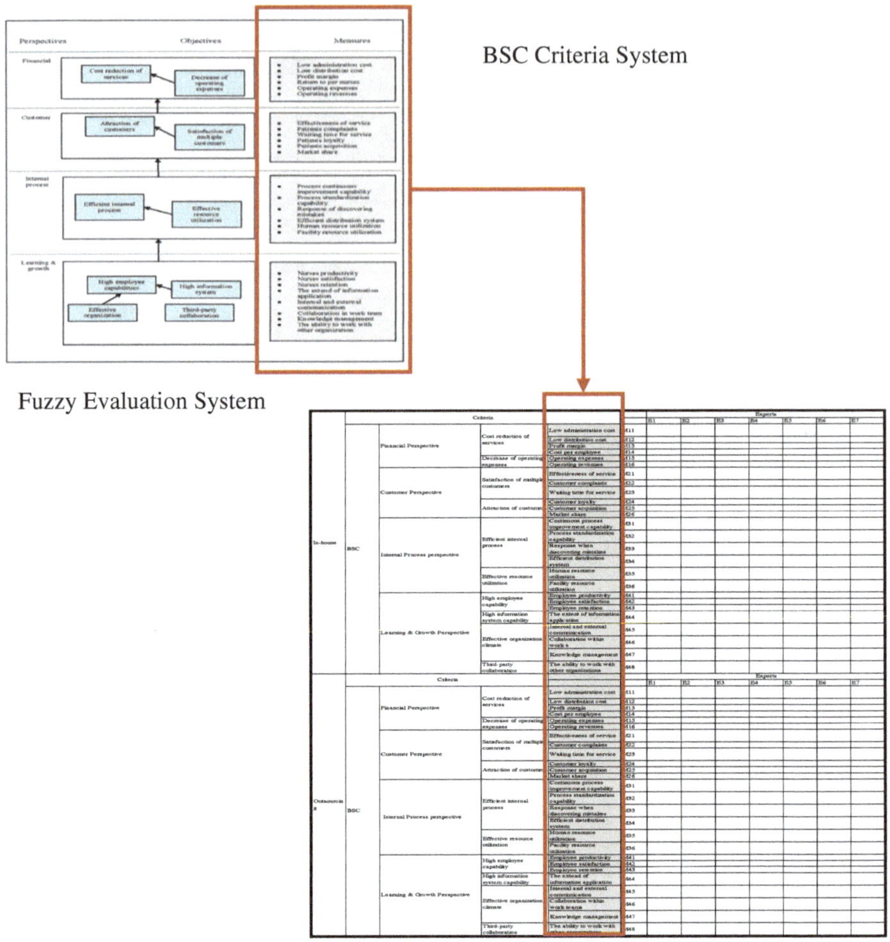

Fig. 7.6 The development of fuzzy evaluation

Table 7.6 Experts weights

Experts	E1	E2	E3	E4	E5	E6	E7
Weight	0.15	0.18	0.09	0.12	0.16	0.19	0.11

The non-fuzzy values of performance values in hospital of the in-house and outsourcing, and the weight of importance of each criterion are shown in Figs. 7.7 and 7.8.

Based on Eqs. (6.10–6.12), we can obtain the assessment score for each alternative. The result of the assessment is shown in Table 7.7.

Criteria			Experts						
			E1	E2	E3	E4	E5	E6	E7
			0.15	0.18	0.09	0.12	0.16	0.19	0.11
Financial perspective	M11	Low administration cost	25	25	15	50	15	25	25
	M12	Low distribution cost	50	15	25	50	50	50	25
	M13	Profit margin	25	25	50	25	25	50	25
	M14	Cost per employee	25	25	50	25	25	50	25
	M15	Operating expenses	15	25	25	15	15	25	25
	M16	Operating revenues	25	25	25	15	25	25	25
Customer perspective	M21	Effectiveness of service	15	50	25	15	25	50	50
	M22	Customer complaints	75	50	50	50	75	50	50
	M23	Waiting time for service	25	15	15	15	25	25	25
	M24	Customer loyalty	50	50	50	50	50	50	50
	M25	Customer acquisition	50	25	25	50	50	25	25
	M26	Market share	50	50	50	50	25	50	50
Internal preocess perspective	M31	Continuous process improvement capability	50	25	50	50	50	25	50
	M32	Process standardization capability	75	50	75	50	50	75	50
	M33	Response when discovering mistakes	50	50	50	50	50	50	50
	M34	Efficient distribution system	50	25	50	50	25	50	75
	M35	Human resource utilization	50	25	25	25	50	25	25
	M36	Facility resource utilization	25	25	15	15	25	15	25
Learning & growth perspective	M41	Employee productivity	50	50	75	50	50	50	50
	M42	Employee satisfaction	75	75	50	75	50	75	75
	M43	Employee retention	75	95	75	50	75	95	75
	M44	The extent of information application	50	50	50	50	50	50	50
	M45	Internal and external communication	75	75	75	75	50	75	75
	M46	Collaboration within work teams	75	50	75	50	75	75	50
	M47	Knowledge management	75	50	50	75	50	50	75
	M48	The ability to work with other organization	75	50	75	75	50	50	75

Criteria			Experts						
			E1	E2	E3	E4	E5	E6	E7
			0.15	0.18	0.09	0.12	0.16	0.19	0.11
Financial perspective	M11	Low administration cost	0.5	0.5	0.75	0.75	0.5	0.5	0.75
	M12	Low distribution cost	0.5	0.5	0.5	0.75	0.5	0.5	0.75
	M13	Profit margin	0.95	0.75	0.95	0.75	0.75	0.75	0.95
	M14	Cost per employee	0.75	0.5	0.5	0.75	0.5	0.5	0.75
	M15	Operating expenses	0.75	0.75	0.5	0.75	0.5	0.75	0.75
	M16	Operating revenues	0.75	0.75	0.5	0.75	0.5	0.75	0.75
Customer perspective	M21	Effectiveness of service	0.75	0.95	0.95	0.75	0.95	0.75	0.75
	M22	Customer complaints	0.75	0.5	0.5	0.25	0.5	0.25	0.5
	M23	Waiting time for service	0.95	0.75	0.75	0.95	0.75	0.75	0.5
	M24	Customer loyalty	0.75	0.75	0.5	0.75	0.5	0.75	0.75
	M25	Customer acquisition	0.75	0.75	0.75	0.95	0.75	0.75	0.95
	M26	Market share	0.95	0.75	0.75	0.75	0.95	0.75	0.75
Internal preocess perspective	M31	Continuous process improvement capability	0.95	0.95	0.75	0.75	0.95	0.95	0.75
	M32	Process standardization capability	0.75	0.75	0.95	0.75	0.75	0.75	0.75
	M33	Response when discovering mistakes	0.75	0.5	0.25	0.25	0.5	0.5	0.75
	M34	Efficient distribution system	0.5	0.75	0.75	0.5	0.5	0.5	0.75
	M35	Human resource utilization	0.95	0.75	0.75	0.5	0.5	0.75	0.75
	M36	Facility resource utilization	0.95	0.95	0.75	0.75	0.75	0.95	0.75
Learning & growth perspective	M41	Employee productivity	0.75	0.75	0.5	0.5	0.75	0.75	0.5
	M42	Employee satisfaction	0.95	0.95	0.75	0.95	0.75	0.75	0.75
	M43	Employee retention	0.75	0.95	0.75	0.95	0.75	0.95	0.75
	M44	The extent of information application	0.25	0.5	0.5	0.25	0.75	0.75	0.5
	M45	Internal and external communication	0.75	0.75	0.75	0.5	0.75	0.75	0.75
	M46	Collaboration within work teams	0.75	0.75	0.5	0.75	0.75	0.5	0.75
	M47	Knowledge management	0.5	0.75	0.75	0.5	0.75	0.75	0.5
	M48	The ability to work with other organization	0.5	0.5	0.75	0.5	0.5	0.5	0.5

$$DP_{ij} = DP_{ij}^1 * W_{e1} + DP_{ij}^2 * W_{e2} + \cdots + DP_{ij}^m * W_{em}$$

$$DI_{ij} = DI_{ij}^1 * W_{e1} + DI_{ij}^2 * W_{e2} + \cdots + DI_{ij}^m * W_{em}$$

$$DS = \sum DP_{ij} * DI_{ij}$$

Fig. 7.7 Non-Fuzzy values of performance values in hospital and the weight of importance for each criterion to calculate the evaluation score of in-house sterile goods

Criteria			Experts						
			E1	E2	E3	E4	E5	E6	E7
			0.15	0.18	0.09	0.12	0.16	0.19	0.11
Financial perspective	M11	Low administration cost	75	75	75	95	75	95	75
	M12	Low distribution cost	50	50	75	50	50	75	50
	M13	Profit margin	50	50	75	50	75	50	50
	M14	Cost per employee	50	50	75	50	75	50	50
	M15	Operating expenses	75	75	50	75	75	50	75
	M16	Operating revenues	75	75	75	50	50	75	75
Customer perspective	M21	Effectiveness of service	75	75	50	75	75	75	50
	M22	Customer complaints	50	75	50	75	50	50	75
	M23	Waiting time for service	75	95	75	50	75	95	75
	M24	Customer loyalty	50	50	50	50	50	50	50
	M25	Customer acquisition	95	75	75	95	75	75	75
	M26	Market share	75	75	50	75	50	75	75
Internal preocess perspective	M31	Continuous process improvement capability	75	75	75	50	75	75	75
	M32	Process standardization capability	95	75	50	75	75	95	75
	M33	Response when discovering mistakes	50	50	75	50	50	75	75
	M34	Efficient distribution system	75	50	50	75	75	75	50
	M35	Human resource utilization	75	75	95	75	75	75	95
	M36	Facility resource utilization	95	95	75	75	95	75	75
Learning & growth perspective	M41	Employee productivity	25	25	25	5	50	25	25
	M42	Employee satisfaction	25	25	5	25	25	5	25
	M43	Employee retention	5	25	25	5	25	25	25
	M44	The extent of information application	50	50	50	50	50	50	50
	M45	Internal and external communication	25	25	50	50	50	25	50
	M46	Collaboration within work teams	50	75	75	50	50	75	75
	M47	Knowledge management	50	50	75	75	75	50	75
	M48	The ability to work with other organization	75	75	95	75	75	95	75

$$DP_{ij} = DP_{ij}^{1} * W_{e1} + DP_{ij}^{2} * W_{e2} + \cdots + DP_{ij}^{m} * W_{em}$$

Criteria			Experts						
			E1	E2	E3	E4	E5	E6	E7
			0.15	0.18	0.09	0.12	0.16	0.19	0.11
Financial perspective	M11	Low administration cost	0.5	0.5	0.75	0.75	0.5	0.5	0.75
	M12	Low distribution cost	0.5	0.5	0.5	0.75	0.5	0.5	0.75
	M13	Profit margin	0.95	0.75	0.95	0.75	0.75	0.75	0.95
	M14	Cost per employee	0.75	0.5	0.5	0.75	0.5	0.5	0.75
	M15	Operating expenses	0.75	0.75	0.5	0.75	0.5	0.75	0.75
	M16	Operating revenues	0.75	0.75	0.5	0.75	0.5	0.75	0.75
Customer perspective	M21	Effectiveness of service	0.75	0.95	0.95	0.75	0.95	0.75	0.75
	M22	Customer complaints	0.75	0.5	0.5	0.25	0.5	0.25	0.5
	M23	Waiting time for service	0.95	0.75	0.75	0.95	0.75	0.75	0.5
	M24	Customer loyalty	0.75	0.75	0.5	0.75	0.5	0.75	0.75
	M25	Customer acquisition	0.75	0.75	0.75	0.95	0.75	0.75	0.95
	M26	Market share	0.95	0.75	0.75	0.75	0.95	0.75	0.75
Internal preocess perspective	M31	Continuous process improvement capability	0.95	0.95	0.75	0.75	0.95	0.95	0.75
	M32	Process standardization capability	0.75	0.75	0.95	0.75	0.75	0.75	0.75
	M33	Response when discovering mistakes	0.75	0.5	0.25	0.25	0.5	0.5	0.75
	M34	Efficient distribution system	0.5	0.75	0.75	0.5	0.5	0.5	0.75
	M35	Human resource utilization	0.95	0.75	0.75	0.5	0.5	0.75	0.75
	M36	Facility resource utilization	0.95	0.95	0.75	0.75	0.75	0.95	0.75
Learning & growth perspective	M41	Employee productivity	0.75	0.75	0.5	0.5	0.75	0.75	0.5
	M42	Employee satisfaction	0.95	0.95	0.75	0.95	0.75	0.75	0.75
	M43	Employee retention	0.75	0.95	0.75	0.95	0.75	0.95	0.75
	M44	The extent of information application	0.25	0.5	0.5	0.25	0.75	0.75	0.5
	M45	Internal and external communication	0.75	0.75	0.75	0.5	0.75	0.75	0.75
	M46	Collaboration within work teams	0.75	0.75	0.5	0.75	0.75	0.5	0.75
	M47	Knowledge management	0.5	0.75	0.75	0.5	0.75	0.75	0.5
	M48	The ability to work with other organization	0.5	0.5	0.75	0.5	0.5	0.5	0.5

$$DI_{ij} = DI_{ij}^{1} * W_{e1} + DI_{ij}^{2} * W_{e2} + \cdots + DI_{ij}^{m} * W_{em}$$

$$DS = \sum DP_{ij} * DI_{ij}$$

Fig. 7.8 Non-fuzzy values of performance values in hospital and the weight of importance for each criterion to calculate the evaluation score of outsourcing sterile goods

Table 7.7 Assessment score of in-house and outsourcing

Criteria			Assessment scale	
			In-house	Outsourcing
Financial perspective	M11	Low administration cost	14.79	47.096
	M12	Low distribution cost	21.57525	31.7775
	M13	Profit margin	26.24	46.125
	M14	Cost per employee	19.04	33.46875
	M15	Operating expenses	14.23125	46.75
	M16	Operating revenues	16.3625	46.75
Customer perspective	M21	Effectiveness of service	28.6748	58.52
	M22	Customer complaints	26.565	27.715
	M23	Waiting time for service	16.38415	61.6541
	M24	Customer loyalty	34.375	34.375
	M25	Customer acquisition	28.457	63.9984
	M26	Market share	37.352	55.825
Internal process perspective	M31	Continuous process improvement capability	36.1045	63.792
	M32	Process standardization capability	46.656	61.0944
	M33	Response when discovering mistakes	25.625	30.621875
	M34	Efficient distribution system	26.32875	38.9725
	M35	Human resource utilization	23.2525	56.09
	M36	Facility resource utilization	17.934	72.4192
Learning and growth perspective	M41	Employee productivity	35.0075	17.822
	M42	Employee satisfaction	57.75	16.296
	M43	Employee retention	67.3312	16.6208
	M44	The extent of information application	26	26
	M45	Internal and external communication	51.12	26.64
	M46	Collaboration within work teams	44.03	43.69
	M47	Knowledge management	38.9725	40.61
	M48	The ability to work with other organizations	32.264375	42.1135
DS score			812.423275	1106.83703

The assessment score of outsourcing sterile goods is higher than in-house. The assessment score is based on the experts' opinions of the performance values in hospital of in-house and outsourcing sterile goods and the weight of importance for each criterion. When a hospital wants to make a decision about the outsourcing sterile goods, they must analyze the hospital situation, and allocate the weight of importance according to the hospital strategy. When the hospital aims to reduce cost then the weights of the financial perspective criteria are greater. When the hospital focuses on patients, then the weights of the customer perspective criteria are greater. Therefore, when a hospital wants to make a decision, the result depends upon the decision makers' opinion according to strategy. Since in a complex system like a hospital, the situation changes continuously, therefore the decision makers must return to the previous step to reconsider the problems and strategy during the decision making process.

7.2.3 Evaluation of the Overall Results

The decision making model for resource management in a complex work system begins with the introduction of the complexity of resource management in hospital. Then the decision making process in complex work system is presented. The three main phases' decision making are used to propose the six steps' decision making process for a complex work system, and present the iterative relationship within the decision making process. Lastly a case study is used to evaluate the developed DERESIS. The procedure to develop DERESIS was based on the problem-solving process in SE methodology, from situation analysis, objective formulation, solution search, evaluation, to the decision.

In the system of measures, four perspectives, i.e. financial perspective, customer perspective, the internal process perspective, and the learning and growth perspective, are applied to develop the measures. In Chap. 7 the measures system was developed. There are six criteria within the financial perspective, the customer perspective and the internal process perspective, and eight criteria within the learning and growth perspective. Qualitative and quantitative criteria are included when comparing the alternatives. In a complex work system the measures system is more complicated, so both qualitative and quantitative criteria are necessary.

Using the measures system, the alternatives are compared in order to select the best choice. In a complex work system there is a large amount of information which cannot be assessed precisely. The fuzzy linguistic is a useful tool to deal with the assessment of qualitative information.

Appendix 1: Five Scale Fuzzy Linguistic of Performance Values in Hospital of In-House and Outsourcing Sterile Goods

See Tables 7.8 and 7.9.

Table 7.8 Five scale fuzzy linguistic of performance values in hospital of in-house sterile goods

Criteria			Experts						
			E1	E2	E3	E4	E5	E6	E7
			0.15	0.18	0.09	0.12	0.16	0.19	0.11
Financial perspective	M11	Low administration cost	P	P	VP	F	VP	P	P
	M12	Low distribution cost	F	VP	P	F	F	F	P
	M13	Profit margin	P	P	F	P	P	F	P
	M14	Cost per employee	P	P	F	P	P	F	P
	M15	Operating expenses	VP	P	P	VP	VP	P	P
	M16	Operating revenues	P	P	P	VP	P	P	P
Customer perspective	M21	Effectiveness of service	VP	F	P	VP	P	F	F
	M22	Customer complaints	G	F	F	F	G	F	F
	M23	Waiting times for service	P	VP	VP	VP	P	P	P
	M24	Customer loyalty	F	F	F	F	F	F	F
	M25	Customer acquisition	F	P	P	F	F	P	P
	M26	Market share	F	F	F	F	P	F	F
Internal preocess perspective	M31	Continuous process improvement capability	F	P	F	F	F	P	F
	M32	Process standardization capability	G	F	G	F	F	G	F
	M33	Response when discovering mistakes	F	F	F	F	F	F	F
	M34	Efficient distribution system	F	P	F	F	P	F	G
	M35	Human resource utilization	F	P	P	P	F	P	P
	M36	Facility resource utilization	P	P	VP	VP	P	VP	P

(continued)

Table 7.8 (continued)

Criteria			Experts						
			E1	E2	E3	E4	E5	E6	E7
			0.15	0.18	0.09	0.12	0.16	0.19	0.11
Learning and growth perspective	M41	Employee productivity	F	F	G	F	F	F	F
	M42	Employee satisfaction	G	G	F	G	F	G	G
	M43	Employee retention	G	VG	G	F	G	VG	G
	M44	The extent of information application	F	F	F	F	F	F	F
	M45	Internal and external communication	G	G	G	G	F	G	G
	M46	Collaboration within work teams	G	F	G	F	G	G	F
	M47	Knowledge management	G	F	F	G	F	F	G
	M48	The ability to work with other organizations	G	F	G	G	F	F	G

Table 7.9 Five scale fuzzy linguistic of performance values in hospital of outsourcing sterile goods

Criteria			Experts						
			E1	E2	E3	E4	E5	E6	E7
			0.15	0.18	0.09	0.12	0.16	0.19	0.11
Financial perspective	M11	Low administration cost	G	G	G	VG	G	VG	G
	M12	Low distribution cost	F	F	G	F	F	G	F
	M13	Profit margin	F	F	G	F	G	F	F
	M14	Cost per employee	F	F	G	F	G	F	F
	M15	Operating expenses	G	G	F	G	G	F	G
	M16	Operating revenues	G	G	G	F	F	G	G
Customer perspective	M21	Effectiveness of service	G	G	F	G	G	G	F
	M22	Customer complaints	F	G	F	G	F	F	G
	M23	Waiting times for service	G	VG	G	F	G	VG	G
	M24	Customer loyalty	F	F	F	F	F	F	F
	M25	Customer acquisition	VG	G	G	VG	G	G	G
	M26	Market share	G	G	F	G	F	G	G

(continued)

Table 7.9 (continued)

Criteria			Experts						
			E1	E2	E3	E4	E5	E6	E7
			0.15	0.18	0.09	0.12	0.16	0.19	0.11
Internal preocess perspective	M31	Continuous process improvement capability	G	G	G	F	G	G	G
	M32	Process standardization capability	VG	G	F	G	G	VG	G
	M33	Response when discovering mistakes	F	F	G	F	F	G	G
	M34	Efficient distribution system	G	F	F	G	G	G	F
	M35	Human resource utilization	G	G	VG	G	G	G	VG
	M36	Facility resource utilization	VG	VG	G	G	VG	G	G
Learning and growth perspective	M41	Employee productivity	P	P	P	VP	F	P	P
	M42	Employee satisfaction	P	P	VP	P	P	VP	P
	M43	Employee retention	VP	P	P	VP	P	P	P
	M44	The extent of information application	F	F	F	F	F	F	F
	M45	Internal and external communication	P	P	F	F	F	P	F
	M46	Collaboration within work teams	F	G	G	F	F	G	G
	M47	Knowledge management	F	F	G	G	G	F	G
	M48	The ability to work with other organizations	G	G	VG	G	G	VG	G

Appendix 2: Five Scale Fuzzy Linguistic of Weight of Importance of Each Criterion

See Table 7.10.

Table 7.10 Five scale fuzzy linguistic of weight of importance of each criterion

Criteria			Experts						
			E1	E2	E3	E4	E5	E6	E7
			0.15	0.18	0.09	0.12	0.16	0.19	0.11
Financial perspective	M11	Low administration cost	MI	MI	I	I	MI	MI	I
	M12	Low distribution cost	MI	MI	MI	I	MI	MI	I
	M13	Profit margin	VI	I	VI	I	I	I	VI
	M14	Cost per Employee	I	MI	MI	I	MI	MI	I
	M15	Operating expenses	I	I	MI	I	MI	I	I
	M16	Operating revenues	I	I	MI	I	MI	I	I
Customer perspective	M21	Effectiveness of service	I	VI	VI	I	VI	I	I
	M22	Customer complaints	I	MI	MI	U	MI	U	MI
	M23	Waiting times for service	VI	I	I	VI	I	I	MI
	M24	Customer loyalty	I	I	MI	I	MI	I	I
	M25	Customer acquisition	I	I	I	VI	I	I	VI
	M26	Market share	VI	I	I	I	VI	I	I
Internal process perspective	M31	Continuous process improvement capability	VI	VI	I	I	VI	VI	I
	M32	Process standardization capability	I	I	VI	I	I	I	I
	M33	Response when discovering mistakes	I	MI	U	U	MI	MI	I
	M34	Efficient distribution system	MI	I	I	MI	MI	MI	I
	M35	Human resource utilization	VI	I	I	MI	MI	I	I
	M36	Facility resource utilization	VI	VI	I	I	I	VI	I

(continued)

Table 7.10 (continued)

Criteria			Experts						
			E1	E2	E3	E4	E5	E6	E7
			0.15	0.18	0.09	0.12	0.16	0.19	0.11
Learning and growth perspective	M41	Employee productivity	I	I	MI	MI	I	I	MI
	M42	Employee satisfaction	VI	VI	I	VI	I	I	I
	M43	Employee retention	I	VI	I	VI	I	VI	I
	M44	The extent of information application	U	MI	MI	U	I	I	MI
	M45	Internal and external communication	I	I	I	MI	I	I	I
	M46	Collaboration within work teams	I	I	MI	I	I	MI	I
	M47	Knowledge management	MI	I	I	MI	I	I	MI
	M48	The ability to work with other organizations	MI	MI	I	MI	MI	MI	MI

Appendix 3: Five Scale Fuzzy Number of Performance Values in Hospital of In-House and Outsourcing Sterile Goods

See Tables 7.11 and 7.12.

Appendix 4: Five Scale Fuzzy Number of Weight of Importance of Each Criterion

See Table 7.13.

Table 7.11 Five scale fuzzy number of performance value in hospital of in-house sterile goods

Criteria			Experts						
			E1	E2	E3	E4	E5	E6	E7
			0.15	0.18	0.09	0.12	0.16	0.19	0.11
Financial perspective	M11	Low administration cost	(10,25,40)	(10,25,40)	(0,0,15)	(35,50,65)	(0,0,15)	(10,25,40)	(10,25,40)
	M12	Low distribution cost	(35,50,65)	(0,0,15)	(10,25,40)	(35,50,65)	(35,50,65)	(35,50,65)	(10,25,40)
	M13	Profit margin	(10,25,40)	(10,25,40)	(35,50,65)	(10,25,40)	(10,25,40)	(35,50,65)	(10,25,40)
	M14	Cost per employee	(10,25,40)	(10,25,40)	(35,50,65)	(10,25,40)	(10,25,40)	(35,50,65)	(10,25,40)
	M15	Operating expenses	(0,0,15)	(10,25,40)	(10,25,40)	(0,0,15)	(0,0,15)	(10,25,40)	(10,25,40)
	M16	Operating revenues	(10,25,40)	(10,25,40)	(10,25,40)	(0,0,15)	(10,25,40)	(10,25,40)	(10,25,40)
Customer perspective	M21	Effectiveness of service	(0,0,15)	(35,50,65)	(10,25,40)	(0,0,15)	(10,25,40)	(35,50,65)	(35,50,65)
	M22	Customer complaints	(60,75,90)	(35,50,65)	(35,50,65)	(35,50,65)	(60,75,90)	(35,50,65)	(35,50,65)
	M23	Waiting times for service	(10,25,40)	(0,0,15)	(0,0,15)	(0,0,15)	(10,25,40)	(10,25,40)	(10,25,40)
	M24	Customer loyalty	(35,50,65)	(35,50,65)	(35,50,65)	(35,50,65)	(35,50,65)	(35,50,65)	(35,50,65)
	M25	Customer acquisition	(35,50,65)	(10,25,40)	(10,25,40)	(35,50,65)	(35,50,65)	(10,25,40)	(10,25,40)
	M26	Market share	(35,50,65)	(35,50,65)	(35,50,65)	(35,50,65)	(10,25,40)	(35,50,65)	(35,50,65)

(continued)

Table 7.11 (continued)

Criteria			Experts						
			E1	E2	E3	E4	E5	E6	E7
			0.15	0.18	0.09	0.12	0.16	0.19	0.11
Internal process perspective	M31	Continuous process improvement capability	(35,50,65)	(10,25,40)	(35,50,65)	(35,50,65)	(35,50,65)	(10,25,40)	(35,50,65)
	M32	Process standardization capability	(60,75,90)	(35,50,65)	(60,75,90)	(35,50,65)	(35,50,65)	(60,75,90)	(35,50,65)
	M33	Response when discovering mistakes	(35,50,65)	(35,50,65)	(35,50,65)	(35,50,65)	(35,50,65)	(35,50,65)	(35,50,65)
	M34	Efficient distribution system	(35,50,65)	(10,25,40)	(35,50,65)	(35,50,65)	(10,25,40)	(35,50,65)	(60,75,90)
	M35	Human resource utilization	(35,50,65)	(10,25,40)	(10,25,40)	(10,25,40)	(35,50,65)	(10,25,40)	(10,25,40)
	M36	Facility resource utilization	(10,25,40)	(10,25,40)	(0,0,15)	(0,0,15)	(10,25,40)	(0,0,15)	(10,25,40)
Learning and growth perspective	M41	Employee productivity	(35,50,65)	(35,50,65)	(60,75,90)	(35,50,65)	(35,50,65)	(35,50,65)	(35,50,65)
	M42	Employee satisfaction	(60,75,90)	(60,75,90)	(35,50,65)	(60,75,90)	(35,50,65)	(60,75,90)	(60,75,90)
	M43	Employee retention	(60,75,90)	(85,100,100)	(60,75,90)	(35,50,65)	(60,75,90)	(85,100,100)	(60,75,90)
	M44	The extent of information application	(35,50,65)	(35,50,65)	(35,50,65)	(35,50,65)	(35,50,65)	(35,50,65)	(35,50,65)

(continued)

Table 7.11 (continued)

Criteria			Experts						
			E1	E2	E3	E4	E5	E6	E7
			0.15	0.18	0.09	0.12	0.16	0.19	0.11
	M45	Internal and external communication	(60,75,90)	(60,75,90)	(60,75,90)	(60,75,90)	(35,50,65)	(60,75,90)	(60,75,90)
	M46	Collaboration within work teams	(60,75,90)	(35,50,65)	(60,75,90)	(35,50,65)	(60,75,90)	(60,75,90)	(35,50,65)
	M47	Knowledge management	(60,75,90)	(35,50,65)	(35,50,65)	(60,75,90)	(35,50,65)	(35,50,65)	(60,75,90)
	M48	The ability to work with other organizations	(60,75,90)	(35,50,65)	(60,75,90)	(60,75,90)	(35,50,65)	(35,50,65)	(60,75,90)

Table 7.12 Five scale fuzzy number of performance value in hospital of outsourcing sterile goods

Criteria			Exports						
			El	E2	E3	E4	E5	E6	E7
			0.15	0.18	0.09	0.12	0.16	0.19	0.11
Financial perspective	M 11	Low administration cost	(60,75,90)	(60,75,90)	(60,75,90)	(85,100,100)	(60,75,90)	(85,100,100)	(60,75,90)
	M12	Low distribution cost	(35,50,65)	(35,50,65)	(60,75,90)	(35,50,65)	(35,50,65)	(60,75,90)	(35,50,65)
	M13	Profit margin	(35,50,65)	(35,50,65)	(60,75,90)	(35,50,65)	(60,75,90)	(35,50,65)	(35,50,65)
	M14	Cost per employee	(35,50,65)	(35,50,65)	(60,75,90)	(35,50,65)	(60,75,90)	(35,50,65)	(35,50,65)
	M15	Operating expenses	(60,75,90)	(60,75,90)	(35,50,65)	(60,75,90)	(60,75,90)	(35,50,65)	(60,75,90)
	M16	Operating revenues	(60,75,90)	(60,75,90)	(60,75,90)	(35,50,65)	(35,50,65)	(60,75,90)	(60,75,90)
Customer perspective	M21	Effectiveness of service	(60,75,90)	(60,75,90)	(35,50,65)	(60,75,90)	(60,75,90)	(60,75,90)	(35,50,65)
	M22	Customer complaints	(35,50,65)	(60,75,90)	(35,50,65)	(60,75,90)	(35,50,65)	(35,50,65)	(60,75,90)
	M23	Waiting times for service	(60,75,90)	(85,100,100)	(60,75,90)	(35,50,65)	(60,75,90)	(85,100,100)	(60,75,90)
	M24	Customer loyalty	(35,50,65)	(35,50,65)	(35,50,65)	(35,50,65)	(35,50,65)	(35,50,65)	(35,50,65)
	N425	Customer acquisition	(85,100,100)	(60,75,90)	(60,75,90)	(85,100,100)	(60,75,90)	(60,75,90)	(60,75,90)
	M26	Market share	(60,75,90)	(60,75,90)	(35,50,65)	(60,75,90)	(35,50,65)	(60,75,90)	(60,75,90)

(continued)

Table 7.12 (continued)

Criteria			Exports						
			El	E2	E3	E4	E5	E6	E7
			0.15	0.18	0.09	0.12	0.16	0.19	0.11
Internal process perspective	M31	Continuous process improvement capability	(60,75,90)	(60,75,90)	(60,75,90)	(35,50,65)	(60,75,90)	(60,75,90)	(60,75,90)
	M32	Process standardization capability	(85,100,100)	(60,75,90)	(35,50,65)	(60,75,90)	(60,75,90)	(85,100,100)	(60,75,90)
	M33	Response when discovering mistakes	(35,50,65)	(35,50,65)	(60,75,90)	(35,50,65)	(35,50,65)	(60,75,90)	(60,75,90)
	N434	Efficient distribution system	(60,75,90)	(35,50,65)	(35,50,65)	(60,75,90)	(60,75,90)	(60,75,90)	(35,50,65)
	M35	Human resource utilization	(60,75,90)	(60,75,90)	(85,100,100)	(60,75,90)	(60,75,90)	(60,75,90)	(85,100,100)
	M36	Facility resource utilization	(85,100,100)	(85,100,100)	(60,75,90)	(60,75,90)	(85,100,100)	(60,75,90)	(60,75,90)
Learningand growth Perspective	M41	Employee productivity	(10,25,40)	(10,25,40)	(10,25,40)	(0,0,15)	(35,50,65)	(10,25,40)	(10,25,40)
	M42	Employee satisfaction	(10,25,40)	(10,25,40)	(0,0,15)	(10,25,40)	(10,25,40)	(0,0,15)	(10,25,40)
	M43	Employee retention	(0,0,15)	(10,25,40)	(10,25,40)	(0,0,15)	(10,25,40)	(10,25,40)	(10,25,40)
	M44	The extent of information application	(35,50,65)	(35,50,65)	(35,50,65)	(35,50,65)	(35,50,65)	(35,50,65)	(35,50,65)

(continued)

Table 7.12 (continued)

Criteria			Exports						
			El	E2	E3	E4	E5	E6	E7
			0.15	0.18	0.09	0.12	0.16	0.19	0.11
	M45	Internal and external communication	(10,25,40)	(10,25,40)	(35,50,65)	(35,50,65)	(35,50,65)	(10,25,40)	(35,50,65)
	M46	Collaboration within work	(35,50,65)	(60,75,90)	(60,75,90)	(35,50,65)	(35,50,65)	(60,75,90)	(60,75,90)
	M47	Knowledge management	(35,50,65)	(35,50,65)	(60,75,90)	(60,75,90)	(60,75,90)	(35,50,65)	(60,75,90)
	M48	The ability to work with other organizations	(60,75,90)	(60,75,90)	(85,100,100)	(60,75,90)	(60,75,90)	(85,100,100)	(60,75,90)

Table 7.13 Five scale fuzzy number of weight of importance of each criterion

Criteria			Experts						
			E1	E2	E3	E4	E5	E6	E7
			0.15	0.18	0.09	0.12	0.16	0.19	0.11
Financial perspective	M11	Low administration cost	(0.35,0.5,0.65)	(0.35,0.5,0.65)	(0.6,0.75,0.9)	(0.6,0.75,0.9)	(0.35,0.5,0.65)	(0.35,0.5,0.65)	(0.6,0.75,0.9)
	M12	Low distribution cost	(0.35,0.5,0.65)	(0.35,0.5,0.65)	(0.35,0.5,0.65)	(0.6,0.75,0.9)	(0.35,0.5,0.65)	(0.35,0.5,0.65)	(0.6,0.75,0.9)
	M13	Profit margin	(0.85,1,1)	(0.6,0.75,0.9)	(0.85,1,1)	(0.6,0.75,0.9)	(0.6,0.75,0.9)	(0.6,0.75,0.9)	(0.85,1,1)
	M14	Cost per employee	(0.6,0.75,0.9)	(0.35,0.5,0.65)	(0.35,0.5,0.65)	(0.6,0.75,0.9)	(0.35,0.5,0.65)	(0.35,0.5,0.65)	(0.6,0.75,0.9)
	M15	Operating expenses	(0.6,0.75,0.9)	(0.6,0.75,0.9)	(0.35,0.5,0.65)	(0.6,0.75,0.9)	(0.35,0.5,0.65)	(0.6,0.75,0.9)	(0.6,0.75,0.9)
	M16	Operating revenues	(0.6,0.75,0.9)	(0.6,0.75,0.9)	(0.35,0.5,0.65)	(0.6,0.75,0.9)	(0.35,0.5,0.65)	(0.6,0.75,0.9)	(0.6,0.75,0.9)
Customer perspective	M21	Effectiveness of service	(0.6,0.75,0.9)	(0.85,1,1)	(0.85,1,1)	(0.6,0.75,0.9)	(0.85,1,1)	(0.6,0.75,0.9)	(0.6,0.75,0.9)
	M22	Customer complaints	(0.6,0.75,0.9)	(0.35,0.5,0.65)	(0.35,0.5,0.65)	(0.1,0.25,0.4)	(0.35,0.5,0.65)	(0.1,0.25,0.4)	(0.35,0.5,0.65)
	M23	Waiting times for service	(0.85,1,1)	(0.6,0.75,0.9)	(0.6,0.75,0.9)	(0.85,1,1)	(0.6,0.75,0.9)	(0.6,0.75,0.9)	(0.35,0.5,0.65)
	M24	Customer loyalty	(0.6,0.75,0.9)	(0.6,0.75,0.9)	(0.35,0.5,0.65)	(0.6,0.75,0.9)	(0.35,0.5,0.65)	(0.6,0.75,0.9)	(0.6,0.75,0.9)
	M25	Customer acquisition	(0.6,0.75,0.9)	(0.6,0.75,0.9)	(0.6,0.75,0.9)	(0.85,1,1)	(0.6,0.75,0.9)	(0.6,0.75,0.9)	(0.85,1,1)
	M26	Market share	(0.85,1,1)	(0.6,0.75,0.9)	(0.6,0.75,0.9)	(0.6,0.75,0.9)	(0.85,1,1)	(0.6,0.75,0.9)	(0.6,0.75,0.9)
Internal process perspective	M31	Continuous process improvement capability	(0.85,1,1)	(0.85,1,1)	(0.6,0.75,0.9)	(0.6,0.75,0.9)	(0.85,1,1)	(0.85,1,1)	(0.6,0.75,0.9)
	M32	Process standardization capability	(0.6,0.75,0.9)	(0.6,0.75,0.9)	(0.85,1,1)	(0.6,0.75,0.9)	(0.6,0.75,0.9)	(0.6,0.75,0.9)	(0.6,0.75,0.9)
	M33	Response when discovering mistakes	(0.6,0.75,0.9)	(0.35,0.5,0.65)	(0.1,0.25,0.4)	(0.1,0.25,0.4)	(0.35,0.5,0.65)	(0.35,0.5,0.65)	(0.6,0.75,0.9)
	M34	Efficient distribution system	(0.35,0.5,0.65)	(0.6,0.75,0.9)	(0.6,0.75,0.9)	(0.35,0.5,0.65)	(0.35,0.5,0.65)	(0.35,0.5,0.65)	(0.6,0.75,0.9)

(continued)

Table 7.13 (continued)

Criteria			Experts						
			E1	E2	E3	E4	E5	E6	E7
			0.15	0.18	0.09	0.12	0.16	0.19	0.11
	M35	Human resource utilization	(0.85,1,1)	(0.6,0.75,0.9)	(0.6,0.75,0.9)	(0.35,0.5,0.65)	(0.35,0.5,0.65)	(0.6,0.75,0.9)	(0.6,0.75,0.9)
	M36	Facility resource utilization	(0.85,1,1)	(0.85,1,1)	(0.6, 0.75,0.9)	(0.6,0.75,0.9)	(0.6,0.75,0.9)	(0.85,1,1)	(0.6,0.75,0.9)
Learning and growth perspective	M41	Employee productivity	(0.6,0.75,0.9)	(0.6,0.75,0.9)	(0.35,0.5,0.65)	(0.35,0.5,0.65)	(0.6,0.75,0.9)	(0.6,0.75,0.9)	(0.35,0.5,0.65)
	M42	Employee satisfaction	(0.85,1,1)	(0.85,1,1)	(0.6,0.75,0.9)	(0.85,1,1)	(0.6,0.75,0.9)	(0.6,0.75,0.9)	(0.6,0.75,0.9)
	M43	Employee retention	(0.6,0.75,0.9)	(0.85,1,1)	(0.6,0.75,0.9)	(0.85,1,1)	(0.6,0.75,0.9)	(0.85,1,1)	(0.6,0.75,0.9)
	M44	The extent of information application	(0.1,0.25,0.4)	(0.35,0.5,0.65)	(0.35,0.5,0.65)	(0.1,0.25,0.4)	(0.6,0.75,0.9)	(0.6,0.75,0.9)	(0.35,0.5,0.65)
	M45	Internal and external communication	(0.6,0.75,0.9)	(0.6,0.75,0.9)	(0.6,0.75,0.9)	(0.35,0.5,0.65)	(0.6,0.75,0.9)	(0.6,0.75,0.9)	(0.6,0.75,0.9)
	M46	Collaboration within work teams	(0.6,0.75,0.9)	(0.6,0.75,0.9)	(0.35,0.5,0.65)	(0.6,0.75,0.9)	(0.6,0.75,0.9)	(0.35,0.5,0.65)	(0.6,0.75,0.9)
	M47	Knowledge management	(0.35,0.5,0.65)	(0.6,0.75,0.9)	(0.6,0.75,0.9)	(0.35,0.5,0.65)	(0.6,0.75,0.9)	(0.6,0.75,0.9)	(0.35,0.5,0.65)
	M48	The ability to work with other organizations	(0.35,0.5,0.65)	(0.35,0.5,0.65)	(0.6,0.75,0.9)	(0.35,0.5,0.65)	(0.35,0.5,0.65)	(0.35,0.5,0.65)	(0.35,0.5,0.65)

References

GGH. (2011). *Guangdong General Hospital.* Retrieved September 4, 2013, from http://www.e5413.com/EN/Info/Info_index.php?ID=1&BID=0&TID=0&page=1

Shimshak, D. G., Lenard, M. L., & Klimberg, R. K. (2009). Incorporating quality into data envelopment analysis of nursing home performance: A case study. *Omega, 37*, 672–685.

Chapter 8
Discussion

The discussions in the following section are the most important results of this work. It includes the discussion of the methodology (see Chap. 3), and the discussion of the result in this book (Chaps. 6 and 7), also discussion of the strengths and weaknesses and the transferability of this study.

8.1 Discussion of the Methodology

The general problem-solving approach from SE according to Haberfellner et al. (1997) is orientated to designing an appropriate methodology as systematically as possible to develop the model which corresponds to the study's problem and objectives. At the beginning of this work the problem of resource management in complex work systems, especially in hospitals was presented, then an additional analysis of the situation from four different perspectives was proposed, system-oriented, cause-oriented, future-oriented, and solution-oriented. We proposed the solution with the development of DERESIS model based on those four perspectives.

The objective of the situation analysis was to detect the study area "the complexity of resource management in hospitals using the example of sterile goods management". The study area was analyzed and defined according to the four perspectives. In addition to this, the documented reports in scientific publications and the analysis of sterile goods in hospitals were used and evaluated systematically. The publications were researched in scientific databases with relevant keywords and keyword combinations; the selection was made according to up to date and relevant contents. The results have been formatted and structured, taking account of complexity.

After the situation analysis, the solutions finding, concept synthesis and analysis were deduced. The main objective was to develop a range of solutions for "resource management in complex work systems". A comprehensive review of literatures

Q. Lin, *Analysis of Resource Management in Complex Work Systems*,
DOI 10.1007/978-981-10-2170-1_8

about the knowledge of research was conducted to find the solution. This was also researched in specialized databases, with relevant keywords and keyword combinations, according to the disciplines. The selection was made by current content relevance. Against this background, the synthesis and further development of knowledge of a model of decision making was made for resource management in complex work systems: the DERESIS model. In this book, the models were proposed from three levels: general framework, generic model, and specific model for sterile goods management in hospital. Because of the complexity of the DERESIS model, it is useful to adopt a multi- or interdisciplinary approach to develop and synthesize the model. The consideration of several disciplines seems elaborate but it is essential in this complex situation. This structure guarantees a high level of comprehensibility and effectiveness of the developed model as well as the implementation generated. With the aid of this model, the implementation could be developed in conjunction with the problems identified in the preliminary study and the requirements resulting from these problems.

The last part was evaluation. The aim was to check systematically and comprehensively the feasibility and suitability of the implementation. The conclusion of the developed model in Chap. 6 was drawn from the knowledge gained. The implementation realized was based on a case study. The model was examined by a hospital which wants to decide whether or not to outsource the sterile goods. The main evaluations were the BSC for criteria development in DERESIS and fuzzy linguistic for assessment design in DERESIS. The evaluation was conducted using a qualitative and quantitative survey from a group of experts. The evaluation approach is appropriate for this stage of the development. Suggestions for criticism and improvement could be considered in a later version.

To summarize, it is found that the methodology could be used to cope with the complex problem and objectives. The division into several steps, i.e. situation analysis, concept synthesis and analysis, and evaluation and decision, which are based on the problem solving cycle of SE, allows a structured approach for analyzing complex issues. The combination of qualitative and quantitative methods has proved again and again to be successful for the processing of ergonomic problems in the past. Against the background of the study, this approach seems particularly suitable for this work.

8.2 Discussion of the Results

In the situation analysis, it is appropriate to detect and delineate holistically the investigation area “resource management in complex work system on the example of sterile goods management in hospital”. The analysis shows that the efficiency and effectiveness of resource utilization is very important for the hospital development and outsourcing is a growing trend in hospital management. However, outsourcing could also have negative effects. Therefore, the decision as to whether or not to outsource is important for hospital development. Sterile goods are very important for the surgical department. Cost reduction in sterile goods management will free up money for the improvement of primary processes directly related to the cure and care of patients.

Against this background, the "***DE**cision Making Model for **RE**source Management of Complex Work **S**ystem **I**n **S**terile Goods Management—DERESIS*" is proposed. Based on the traditional Simon three phases' decision making process, the six steps decision making process is proposed, and the three levels of the DERESIS model are also presented: general framework, generic model, and specific model.

The DERESIS model is evaluated in a hospital which wants to decide whether or not to outsource the sterile goods. So the alternatives of the case study are in-house and outsourcing sterile goods. At this stage, the evaluation is focused on criteria system development and assessment system design.

8.2.1 Discussion of the Decision Making Process

Decision making is the process of generating and evaluating selected alternatives and making choices from them. In order to come up with the best choice in a complex work system, it may necessary to go through the decision making process repeatedly. In the decision making process, each step needs to be revisited for refinement, or return to the previous step for additional processing. Therefore, the decision making process is not structured in a strictly orderly manner; it is iterative and cyclical process.

Decision making for resource management in complex work systems is often complicated, as there are numerous components and interconnections in complex work systems, and the situation changes continuously and discontinuously, and the available information can be potentially ambiguous. Decision making in complex work systems can be a networked process. Theoretical concepts of networked thinking can be applied to analyze and evaluate the complex processes of decision making. Networked thinking can make complexity easier to handle and create new ideas.

In the developed DERESIS model, there are some iterative relationships. The whole process is treated not in a linear manner, but as an iterative and networked process. In this step of the process, it is necessary to return to the previous step to obtain more information or reconsider strategies.

8.2.2 Discussion of Criteria Development

A decision cannot be made by using a single criterion in complex work systems. The decision makers have to deal with multiple alternatives with multiple criteria. And the criteria must be identified and considered systematically. Multiple criteria decision making can support the logical and systematic process of evaluating all possible alternatives and choosing the best one (Malakooti 2011). In this study, we proposed the BSC to develop the criteria system for decision making.

The BSC is a multidimensional measured performance for making strategic decisions. It established the qualitative and quantitative measures for decision making from four perspectives, i.e. financial, customer, internal process, and learning and growth perspectives. The proposed BSC approach contains financial, as well as non-financial performance indicators. It can examine the quality of the services provided, the satisfaction of internal and external customers, the self-improvement system of the organization, and the ability of the organization to adapt and change (Grigoroudis et al. 2012). The measurement system in the BSC is a powerful tool for enabling complex decision making by a management team (Gordon et al. 1998).

The development of such a scorecard system is of great importance, because it is able to describe the vision of the hospital, to align departments, units, employees in the achievement of common goals, and to focus on the most important improvement efforts. It focuses not only a single aspect of the hospital, but also seeks to translate strategic objectives into a coherent set of performance measures. The BSC can provide solutions to increasingly complex resource management problems, and help to improve the quality of decisions by making them more explicit, rational and efficient.

Outsourcing sterile goods has significance to hospital development. As a result, it has become a strategic option for a hospital seeking to improve overall performance (Lee et al. 2003). The outsourcing objectives are not only economic, but also strategic, technological and social (Tjader et al. 2013). Therefore, the BSC approach was used to consider the elements of decision making and structure within the criteria system.

In the case study of this book, the BSC employs 26 measures for hospital performance: 6 measures in financial perspective, 6 measures in customer perspective, 6 measures in internal process perspective, and 8 measures in learning and growth perspective. According to this measurement system, the in-house and outsourced sterile goods will be compared in order to decide which is better for the overall performance of the hospital.

BSC can establish the financial and non-financial measures for decision making, but there exist some limitations to the BSC. It does not guarantee the inclusion of every measure in all of the dimensions, and the final selection of measures is left to the decision makers. Against this background, group research is applied to establish the measurement system. The group of experts includes multidisciplinary experts can give a comprehensive view, and this overcomes the decision makers' subjective consciousness.

8.2.3 Discussion of the Fuzzy Linguistic Assessment

During the decision making process, a finite number of alternatives are to be evaluated against a set of criteria to select the desired one. The desired/best alternative is usually selected by making comparisons between alternatives with respect to each criterion. There is a large amount of information which cannot be assessed precisely in a quantitative form, but may be possible in a qualitative one, when comparing the alternatives during the decision making process. Decision making in complex work systems involves complex, ambiguous, and vague phenomena. Therefore, in this study, the fuzzy linguistic approach provided a mathematical framework to describe the subjective assessment of alternatives versus criteria, and the importance of weighting the criteria.

The use of fuzzy linguistic models in decision making is highly useful when the performance values cannot be expressed by means of numerical values. The fuzzy linguistic approach gives a more flexible framework, which allows us to represent the information in a more direct and adequate way, and then convert the qualitative information into quantitative information. Decision makers can express their judgments more realistically, and assess the alternatives more easily. The fuzzy linguistic decision making is an appropriate tool to model qualitative information in multiple real-world decision situations.

In this book, fuzzy linguistics theory was used to evaluate the alternatives based on the selected criteria and the importance of weighting the criteria. The alternatives are in-house and outsourcing sterile goods in hospitals. Firstly, the experts express their opinion of each alternative for the overall performance of the hospital. The fuzzy linguistic terms are: very poor, poor, fair, good, and very good. Then the experts express their judgments for the importance of weighting each criterion. The fuzzy linguistic terms for the importance weighting are: absolutely unimportant, unimportant, moderately important, important, and very important. After the fuzzy linguistic evaluation, the defuzzification procedure was proposed to convert the fuzzy value into a numerical value in order to compare the assessment results, and make a decision.

The linguistic approach aims to solve complicated, subjective and undefined situations. It provides a framework with more human consistency than is usual, and helps the development of decision processes.

8.3 Strengths and Weaknesses of This Study

8.3.1 Strengths of the Study

(A) **Multi-measures in BSC**

In the BSC both the short and long term objectives, financial and non-financial measures, and external and internal measures provide a much more holistic view of the state of the organization. It establishes relationships between and within different dimensions and measures. The framework of BSC captures different perspectives and measures, and provides managers with a fast and comprehensive overview of their organizations for strategic analysis. BSC is a suitable method for developing a measures system in a complex work system.

(B) **Quantitative and Qualitative Assessment**

The resource decision making in a complex work system is a very difficult and complex work. It involves more qualitative information. There is not sufficient data for the qualitative information. With the multi-measures system in BSC, most non-financial measures are qualitative by nature, and often depend upon experts' judgment. Such factors involve a great degree of linguistic deficiency (Klir et al. 1997). Fuzzy linguistic evaluation is flexible enough for situations where fuzzy and non-fuzzy assessments are necessary. It allows data to be taken in linguistic terms. This provides more realistic, accurate and reliable decision models.

In this book, the BSC was proposed to develop the multi-measures system, and fuzzy linguistic was used to evaluate the performance values and the weight of importance of each measure. This enables the experts to express their judgments more realistically, and can help to convert the subjective cognition into an information entity. After the defuzzification, we can obtain the quantitative data for evaluation. This is convenient for comparing the alternatives and selecting a choice. Therefore, the quantitative and qualitative assessment is of benefit when making a decision in a complex work system.

(C) **Wide Range of Application**

The model developed in this study aims to develop a decision making model for resource management of complex work systems using the example of sterile goods management in hospitals. The implementation of this model is undertaken in a hospital which wants to make a decision about in-house or outsourcing sterile goods. The alternatives for the implementation are therefore in-house and outsourcing. However, this model can be used in decision making for other issues. The decision making process described in Chap. 6 could be used here. After the identification of alternatives the BSC and fuzzy linguistic evaluation can be used to compare alternatives. The BSC with fuzzy linguistic to assess alternatives in decision making can be used with decision making in complex systems, where the evaluation data is unavailable or unreliable.

(D) **Systems Engineering Approach for Development of DERESIS**

In this book, the SE approach was used to develop the DERESIS model. SE focuses on the design and control of system activities to meet objectives. It is a problem-solving methodology for designing and configuring systems. The problem-solving process contains several steps for systematically analyzing. The search for solutions was seemed as an iterative process (Schönsleben 2013). The problem solving process in SE provides a methodology to carry out the research.

8.3.2 *Weaknesses of the Study*

(A) **Measures are not Comprehensive**

The measures proposed are based on four perspectives in BSC, i.e. financial perspective, customer perspective, internal process perspective, and learning and growth perspective. From the various dimensions of BSC, managers can have a complete picture of organizational performance, and develop a relatively comprehensive measures system. But the final selection of measures which are included depends upon the decision makers. Hence it does not guarantee the inclusion of every measure in all of the dimensions. It needs more discussion and research to develop the comprehensive measures system for decision making.

(B) **Subjectivity of Decision Makers**

In the measures system development, workshops were held to discuss and identify the measures within each perspective. And in the assessment system design, the performance values, and the weight of importance of each criterion in each perspective, were evaluated by the experts. Although the experts included hospital managers, clinical staff, and academics, it achieved a relatively comprehensive view for assessing the alternatives. But the assessment was based on the opinion of experts; the subjectivity of these experts was unavoidable.

(C) **Universality of the Model is still to be Verified**

In this book, we proposed a theoretical DERESIS model from three levels: general framework, generic model, and specific model. Then we used a case study to evaluate whether the developed model was suitable and sufficiently flexible for decision making for outsourcing sterile goods in hospitals, and to what extent the developed model can be implemented realistically.

The case study was undertaken in a hospital which wanted to make a decision about in-house or outsourcing sterile goods. In the future, the theoretical model should be implemented in a more complex system to verify its suitability and scientific value. Therefore, the universality of the DERESIS needs to be verified.

8.4 Transferability

The main objective of this study is to develop the decision making process for resource management in complex work systems, using the example of outsourcing sterile goods decision making. This is a strategic option for a hospital seeking to improve its overall performance. The development process of this model has advantages for other strategic outsourcing decision making.

Although the focus in this study is outsourcing sterile goods decision making in hospitals, other outsourcing decision making in hospitals is also a strategic option for hospital development. Therefore, the contribution of this study is not only useful for the outsourcing sterile goods decision, but also for other outsourcing decision making in hospitals. An example of this would be the outsourcing of the IT service, human resources, medical devices, et al. Also the model is useful for other outsourcing decision making in complex work systems. With the pressure of globalization, rapid technological evolution, and the necessity for cost reduction, organizations are faced with the decisions about outsourcing. Outsourcing has become a strategic option for organizations seeking to improve their overall business performance (Lee et al. 2003). The decision about outsourcing is important for the development of organizations.

After the choice whether or not to outsource, the next step is to implement the outsourcing strategy. In this study, there are no discussions about this implementation. The next step would be to undertake research into implementing outsourcing. It would involve vender selection, standardization, laws and regulations, network of outsourcing, et al.

The model developed in this study is also suitable for decision making in other fields, which are complex, and where it is difficult to obtain precise evaluation information.

References

Gordon, D., Chapman, R., Kunov, H., Dolan, A., & Carter, M. (1998). Hospital management decision surport: A balanced scorecard approach. *Studies Health Technology and Informatics, 52*(1), 453–456.

Grigoroudis, E., Orfanoudaki, E., & Zopounidis, C. (2012). Strategic performance measurement in a healthcare organization: A multiple criteria approach based on balanced scorecard. *Omega, 40*(1), 104–119.

Haberfellner, R., Nagel, P., Becker, M., Büchel, A., & von Massow, H. (1997). *Systems engineering: Methodik und Praxis. 9. Verbesserte Auflage* (W. F. Daenzer, & F. Huber, Hrsg.). Zuerich: Verl. Industrielle Organisation.

Klir, G. J., Wang, Z., & Harmanec, D. (1997). Constructing fuzzy measures in expert systems. *Fuzzy Sets and Systems, 92*(2), 251–264.

Lee, J. N., Huynh, M. Q., Kwok, C. W., & Pi, S. M. (2003). IT outsourcing evolution: Past, present and future. *Communications of the ACM, 46*(5), 84–89.

Malakooti, B. (2011). Systematic decision process for intelligent decision making. *Journal of Intelligent Manufacturing, 22*(4), 627–642.

Schönsleben, T. (2013). *Systems engineering methodology*. Retrieved May 24, 2013, from http://www.timgroup.ethz.ch/education/Courses_at_TIMGROUP/spring_2013/SE_FS_2013_final.pdf

Tjader, Y. X., May, J. H., Shang, J., Vargas, L. G., & Gao, N. (2013). Firm-level outsourcing decision making: A balanced scorecard-based analytic network process model. *International Journal of Production Economics,*. doi:10.1016/j.ijpe.2013.04.017

Chapter 9
Future Research

Many countries need to be concerned with the effects of demographic change on various levels in the coming years, both in the economy and within society. Hospitals, as one component of health care service organizations, have recognized the pressures to control costs and to demonstrate the value of the services delivered. They are now seeking new paradigms to improve the efficiency and effectiveness of resource utilization (Shortell and Kaluzny 2000). The provision of health care services involves making decisions about the planning and management of resources (Harper 2002). Although the decision making model has been researched over recent decades, decision making in complex systems requires techniques and scientific methods to make well-informed decisions about the trade-off between cost and quality. There is a need to deal with the quantitative and qualitative information during the decision making process. There is much research into resource management in primary and secondary work processes in hospital. However, resources management in tertiary processes receives little attention.

The model developed in this work can provide a conceptual framework for a decision making model, based on multi-criteria and quantitative and qualitative assessment in complex systems, using the example of sterile goods, which belong to the tertiary process in hospitals. It can give the decision makers a more holistic view of the organization's strategy. Moreover it can help to solve the difficult problems in decision making where there is not complete and precise data.

The following steps should be considered to improve and perfect the developed DERESIS model:

- To generalize the model. The developed DERESIS model should be applied in more hospital systems to demonstrate its feasibility, and identify opportunities for improvement.
- Effective tools could be developed to support decision making in complex work systems.

Q. Lin, *Analysis of Resource Management in Complex Work Systems*,
DOI 10.1007/978-981-10-2170-1_9

- Vender selection should be taken into account when making decisions about the outsourcing of sterile goods. Furthermore, the legal and organizational framework for supply of these goods should be discussed.
- There should be further implementation of these concepts to other fields.

References

Harper, P. R. (2002). A framework for operational modeling of hospital resources. *Health Care Management Science, 5*, 165–173.

Shortell, S. M., & Kaluzny, A. D. (2000). Organization theory and health services management. In S. M. Shortell & A. D. Kaluzny (Eds.), *Health care management: Organization design and behavior* (4th ed.). New York: Delma.

Glossary

Alternative The alternative refers to one of a number of things from which to choose

BSC It is the Balanced Scorecard

Cause-and-effect relationship It describes a relationship between actions or events, such that one or more are the result of the other or others

Centre-of-area Abbreviation to COA is a defuzzification method

Comprehensive Comprehensive refers to including all details, information, etc. which are needed or are relevant

Cooperation It is the process of groups of organisms working together for their common benefit

CSSD It is the Central Sterile Supply Department, which is an integrated place in hospitals and other health care organizations, which performs sterilization and other actions on medical devices, equipment and consumables

Customer acquisition Customer acquisition refers to the process of gaining more new customers

Defuzzification It is the process of producing a quantifiable result in fuzzy logic, given fuzzy sets and corresponding membership degrees

Demographic Demographics are the quantifiable statistics of a given population

DERESIS DERESIS refers to the model which is developed in this thesis to analyze and optimize the resource provision in complex hospital systems: ***DE**cision making model for **RE**source management for complex work **S**ystem **I**n **S**terile goods management*

Dynamic This describes constant change and progress

Effectiveness Effectiveness refers to doing correct things, such as doing the right task, completing activities and achieving goals

Q. Lin, *Analysis of Resource Management in Complex Work Systems*,
DOI 10.1007/978-981-10-2170-1

Efficiency Efficiency refers to doing things in a correct manner; it is the quality of being able to do a task successfully, without wasting time, effort or cost

Fuzzy linguistics Fuzzy linguistics combines the fuzzy sets and modern linguistics. Fuzzy language can be dealt with in a more reasonable and flexible way

General framework It describes the framework as a whole; it is not restricted to any one thing or area

Generic model It describes the model that refers or relates to a whole class of similar things

In-house In-house refers the work or activities which are done by employees of an organization or company, rather than by outside workers

Interconnection Closely connected

Interdependence The relationship in which each member is mutually dependent on others

Interdisciplinary Interdisciplinary involves the combining of two or more academic disciplines into one activity

Iteration It describes the act of repeating a process to achieve a design goal, target or result

Logistics Logistics is handling an operation which involves providing labor and materials to be supplied as needed

Market share The proportion of the total sales of the product which is produced by company

Mean-of-maximum Abbreviation to MOM is a defuzzification method

Multidisciplinary approach Multidisciplinary approach involves drawing appropriately from multiple disciplines to redefine problems and reach solutions

Networked thinking Networked thinking presents a combination of cybernetic and systemic ideas and complexity. It views a system as a network of interrelated effects, leading to emergent behavior of the system as a whole

OT It is the Operating Theatre. It is a facility within a hospital where surgical operations are carried out in a sterile environment

Outsourcing Outsourcing is the contracting out of a business process to a third-party

Performance Performance means that how successful an organization is, or how well something is done

Postoperative infection The infections which occur after surgical procedures

Problem-solving The thought processes involved in solving a problem

Qualitative Qualitative refers to descriptions or distinctions based on some quality or characteristic rather than on some quantity or measured value

Quantitative The term quantitative refers to a type of information based on quantities or quantifiable data

Resource provision The act of giving the resources or making the resource available to people or organizations who need or want it

Specific model It describes the model of a particular area, problem, or subject

Sterile goods The articles which must be sterilized

Sterilization: The procedure of destroying all microorganisms in hospital, or other health care organizations, in order to prevent the spread of infection

Sub-system Sub systems are the smaller systems within a system

Super-system Super system describes an extremely large and complex system

Teamwork Teamwork means several associates working together. Teamwork in health care means a dynamic process involving two or more health care professionals with complementary backgrounds and skills, sharing common goals and exercising concerted physical and mental effort to assess, plan, or evaluate patient care

Third-party collaboration Collaboration with someone or other organization which is not involved in a transaction

Top-down approach Top-down approach refers to breaking down of a system to gain insight into its compositional sub-systems

Transferability The quality of being transferable or exchangeable

Triangular fuzzy number Triangular fuzzy number is a fuzzy number represented by three points

Universality The universality describes an application can be used widely

Utilization The act of using

Work system A work system is a system in which human participants and machines perform work using information, technology, and other resources to produce products and services for internal or external customers

FSC
www.fsc.org
MIX
Papier | Fördert
gute Waldnutzung
FSC® C083411

Kolibri 360 GmbH
Ferdinand-Jühlke-Straße 7
99095 Erfurt, Deutschland
produktsicherheit@kolibri360.de